OUR BIRD COMRADES

By

LEANDER S. KEYSER

Author of "Birddom," "In Bird Land," and "Birds of the Rockies," etc.

Rand, McNally & Company Chicago New York London

The Rand-McNally Press Chicago

To: ALL WHO LOVE THE BIRDS FOR THEIR OWN SAKES, who desire to cultivate comradeship with them in books and in the field, and who will study them with the glass and without the gun.

BY WAY OF INTRODUCTION

To know the birds intimately, to interpret their lives in all their varied conditions, one must get close to them. For the purpose of accomplishing this object the author of this volume has gone to their haunts day after day and watched them persistently at not a little cost of time, effort, and money. While the limits of a single volume do not permit him to present all of his observations, it is hoped that those here offered will be satisfactory as far as they go, and that the reader will be able to glean from these pages some new as well as interesting facts relative to bird life.

The writer has had another purpose in view in preparing this book: He wishes to inspire others, especially the young, to use their eyes and ears in the study of the enchanting volume of Nature. This object, he believes, will be best accomplished by furnishing concrete examples of what may be achieved by earnest research. For purposes of stimulus an ounce of example is worth a pound of precept. If another sees you and me doing a thing joyfully, earnestly, we need scarcely say to him, "Go thou and do likewise."

There is not much in the book that is technical, yet it aims at scientific accuracy in all of its statements, no bird being described whose status in the avian system has not been determined. If strange exploits are sometimes recited, the author has simply to say that he has been veracious in all of his statements, and that all the stories are "true bird stories." The author modestly believes that it will not be found uninteresting to nature lovers in general.

Much of the material included in this volume has previously appeared in various periodicals, to the publishers of which the writer would hereby make grateful acknowledgment for their courtesy in waiving their copyright privileges. A number of the journals are given due credit elsewhere in the book.

THE AUTHOR.

BEGINNING THE STUDY

Why should not people ride natural history hobbies as well as other kinds of hobbies? Almost all persons become interested in some special study, recreation, or pastime, and their choice is not always as profitable as the selection of a specific branch of nature lore would be. The writer confesses that he would rather pursue a bright, lilting bird or butterfly than a bounding tennis-ball or football, and he finds the chase every whit as exciting and the knowledge gained of more permanent value; and he says this without in anywise intending to discountenance healthful games and athletic exercises, but simply to express a preference. What could be more fascinating, for instance, than for a young person--or an older person, either, for that matter--to spend his leisure in trying to identify every bird in his neighborhood? As a result of such an attempt he would doubtless become so interested in the study of his bird neighbors that he would resolve to learn all he could about their charming habits.

How may one study the birds intelligently? That is a question every beginner will want to have answered. When I began my bird studies I spent much valuable time in simply trying to learn the modus operandi, and while I do not consider the time thus spent entirely wasted, still I am anxious to save my readers as much needless effort as possible. This I shall do by showing them how they may begin at once to form an acquaintance with the various families and species of birds.

It goes without saying that, to become a successful nature student, one must have good eyes, strong limbs, nimble feet, and, above all, an alert mind. People who lack these qualities, especially the last, will not be likely to pursue the noble science of ornithology. The stupid sort will prefer to drowse in the shade, and the light-minded will care only for the gay round of social pleasures. Any bright and earnest person, however, can in good time become an expert student of the feathered creation, provided only that he feels a genuine interest in such pursuit. No one, let it be repeated, can study nature successfully in a dull, perfunctory spirit. Here, as in religion, one must have the baptism of fire, the temper of devotion.

In the study of birds it must be admitted that men and boys have some advantage over their cousins of the gentler sex. Men folk may ramble pretty much where they please without danger, whereas the freedom of women folk in this respect is somewhat restricted. However, the engaging works of Mrs. Olive Thorne Miller, of Mrs. Florence M. Bailey, and of many others prove that women are not debarred from outdoor studies, and that in some ways they may even have an advantage over men; they are not so ambitious to cover a wide territory, to penetrate to out-of-the-way haunts, or to roll up a long "list," and they are therefore apt to make more intimate studies of the common species, thus getting into the very heart of the bird's life. A man's observations may embrace a wider range, and he may add more species to the science of ornithology than his sister, but she will be likely to discover facts about the commonest fowl that he will overlook. The study of birds, therefore, offers a fascinating field for girls and women as well as for their brothers.

What tools are needed for acquiring bird lore? To begin at the beginning, let me ask: Who would expect to study the plants and flowers without a botany? or the rocks and fossils and the general structure of the earth without a reliable work on geology? or the planets and stars without a treatise on astronomy? So, if you desire a knowledge of ornithology, you will need what is known as a bird "key," or "manual," or "handbook"--that is, a scientific work that shows how the birds have been classified, with accurate descriptions of all the families, genera, species, subspecies, and varieties, together with the common and scientific names of all the species and brief accounts of their ranges and general habits. When you have found a plant or a flower that is new to you, what is your first task? To "run it down" in a botanical key. Just so, having found a feathered stranger, you should note its markings, shape, size, etc., and then "run it down" with the aid of a bird manual. It is much better to run a bird down in this way than to shoot it down.

It is pertinent to say at this time that no one should disparage scientific treatises, or the learned and painstaking people who gather the material for them and prepare them. It is quite the fashion nowadays, when a "popular" book on birds appears, for some reviewers to compare it with the so-called "dry" scientific works of the specialists, to the disparagement of the latter. This is as wrong as it is gratuitous. The "popular" book, delightful as it may be, could not have been written, or, if written, would have had little real value, had it not been for the help obtained from the systematists, who, with almost infinite toil, have made possible the scientific classification of the numerous members of the bird tribe. Pioneer work in ornithology, as elsewhere, may not be very enchanting to most people, but it is necessary. The scientific spirit should be honored, not disdained, for without it accuracy would be impossible. On the other hand, the man who plods with scientific details should not look with contempt upon the man who popularizes the results of technical study by giving it an attractive literary setting. In short, the scientific writer and the "popular" writer are alike worthy of "honorable mention," for both of them are needful factors in the dissemination of knowledge.

You will want to know where a first-rate bird manual can be obtained. It affords me sincere pleasure to recommend two works of the kind that cover the entire avian field for residents of the United States. They are new, up-to-date, and convenient. To those who live east of the Mississippi River I would commend Mr. Frank M. Chapman's "Handbook of Birds of Eastern North America." The best praise I can bestow upon this book is to assure you that it will give entire satisfaction as a handbook. Happily another manual (Mrs. Florence M. Bailey's "Handbook of Birds of the Western United States") was recently issued, treating the avifauna west of the Mississippi just as thoroughly as Mr. Chapman's work deals with that of the eastern part of our country. Both books contain lavish illustrations by expert and accurate bird artists--a feature that is invaluable in the work of identification. They possess a further advantage in not being too large to be carried with you in your excursions afield, enabling you to name each feathered stranger on the spot.

Should you desire a single volume that will help you to identify any bird you may meet on our continent, I would urge you to secure the latest revised edition of Dr. Elliott Coues's "Key to North American Birds." It is fully illustrated, thoroughly scientific and up-to-date in the matter of classification, and yet not too technical for practical use. This book is too bulky to be carried with you to the haunts of the birds, but it may be used in this way: Note carefully the markings and other peculiarities of each new bird you meet; then, as soon as you return home, while all the circumstances are fresh in your memory, consult your "key" and make sure, if possible, of the identity of all your "finds."

Mr. Robert Ridgway, one of the foremost ornithologists of our country, is now preparing a great work which is worthy of the highest praise. It is entitled "The Birds of North and Middle America," and is the most comprehensive work yet undertaken relative to the avifauna of the entire North American Continent, giving a large amount of scientific data respecting all the species. After its completion it will enable the student to identify every bird known to science from the Isthmus of Panama to the far North and from the Atlantic to the Pacific. At this writing two volumes have been issued. They are published under government auspices by the United States National Museum at Washington, D. C., and may be procured perhaps without cost by writing to the secretary of the Smithsonian Institution. Of this the writer cannot be absolutely sure, as the supply of printed copies may be limited.

Nothing more need be said about bird manuals, save to warn you against spending your money for books which describe only a part of the avifauna of a given region and yet are advertised as serviceable for the identification of all birds. Unless you have plenty of money to spend, when you buy a manual buy one that is scientifically accurate and complete. Nothing is more trying to the student of birds, whether tyro or expert, than to encounter a new bird and then fail to find it described or even mentioned in the book that has been foisted upon him as a manual. In saying this I do not mean to discourage the purchase of the charming popular books written in a literary vein and describing personal observations on bird life, such as the works of John Burroughs, Bradford Torrey, Olive Thorne Miller, and many others. These books, however, are not advertised as handbooks, and thus no one is deceived in buying them.

Even with the best manual in hand, you must not expect to be able to identify every new bird at the first attempt, for some species are either exceedingly shy or obscurely marked, or probably both, while quite a number are so much alike in markings and habits that it is hard to distinguish them from one another. A few birds remained enigmas to me for a number of years, in spite of the help of the field glass. At intervals for several months you will often catch provoking glimpses of some nymph-like bird before you succeed in determining its true place in the avian system. But patience and persistence will some day overcome the most stubborn difficulties.

Since the foregoing references to leading bird manuals were written, a new work, which is unique in plan, has been published. I refer to the book entitled "Color Key to North American Birds"; text by Frank M. Chapman, pictures by Chester A. Reed. The range of the volume is from the Atlantic to the Pacific ocean and from the southern boundary of the United States to the far north. It contains a brief description of every species and sub-species within the limits named; a key to all the Orders and Families, with the common and scientific names of all the birds; an introduction to every chief division; and last, and highly important, colored pictures of all the species and many of the geographical varieties. What more can the bird student desire for purposes of identification? While the other manuals give fuller descriptions of habits, songs, etc., and need not, therefore, be superseded by this volume, yet frankness forces us to say that if the student, and especially the beginner, cannot afford to buy more than one bird book, the Chapman-Reed "Color Key" is the one to get. It is of a convenient size for carrying afield, so that a feathered stranger can be identified on the spot. It can be used anywhere in the United States, in British America, and Alaska. Think of that, fellow bird-lovers!

A good field glass is indispensable to successful bird study, especially if you desire to name all the birds without killing any, as I hope you do. Perhaps the older ornithologists, like Audubon and Wilson, did not use helps of this kind, but they used guns, and consequently had to study dead birds, while you and I want to study living ones. Their killing of birds was, indeed, necessary, for purposes of scientific classification; but now that such classifying has, for the most part, been attained, the gun has largely gone out of vogue, and the glass has taken its place. Let your alliterative motto be: With the glass, not the gun.

I would advise you not to buy a flashily colored glass, for it will dazzle your eyes on sunshiny days. Be sure to get one that is easily focused, as you must be quick in studying such shy creatures as the birds. At first the glass may strain and tire your eyes, but that difficulty will pass in a short time. Expertness will soon be won in the use of a binocular, so that you will be able, almost instantly, to get the desired object within its field, even though the object be quite tiny. An opera glass is a great deal better than no glass at all; a field glass is better still, and a Bausch & Lomb binocular of six to eight magnifying power is the best of all; being almost equal to having the bird in hand. The observer must lose as little time as possible in sighting a shy bird, or it may escape him altogether.

A book-bag or haversack, strapped around your shoulders, will also be a convenience. In it you can stow your bird manual, and a luncheon in case you expect to spend the whole day in the open, for a hungry rambler is not likely to be an acute observer. A notebook and a lead pencil, carried in handy pockets, should not be forgotten. Donning an old suit of clothes, you can roam where you will, threading your way through brier and bush, wading the bog or the shallow stream, dropping upon your knees, even flinging yourself upon the ground, to spy upon a wary bird flitting about in the copse.

In almost all kinds of weather I wear rubber boots in my excursions to the haunts of the birds. The observer can never tell when he may have to wade a stream or tramp through a boggy marsh. In wet and cold weather the need of rubber boots can be seen readily, but even in dry and warm weather they have one decided advantage--they do not become slippery on the soles as one tramps through the leaf-strewn woods or the grassy fields. Every pedestrian knows that sole-leather is apt to become as smooth as glass, making it difficult to retain one's footing. On the other hand, rubber seems to cling to the ground, no matter how much it is worn. The only objection to rubbers is that they are uncomfortably warm in hot weather; but that difficulty can be overcome by frequently plunging into a cool stream and standing there for several minutes.

Let me caution you, however, not to purchase a heavy pair of rubber boots. Insist on having a light pair or none at all. A good pair of rubber boots are a real luxury, for with them you may tramp about in all kinds of damp and boggy places without fear of wetting your feet, though it goes without saying that you must be careful not to wade in over the tops of your footgear.

Of great assistance to the pedestrian is a light cane. In climbing Pikes Peak one evening after dark, I doubt whether I should have been able to gain the summit had it not been for my tough little wild-cherry cane, upon which I could lean when almost exhausted, which supported my faltering steps, and which happily never grew weary. Two years later it helped me to scale a number of snow-capped mountains, among them Grays Peak and Peak Number Eight of the Ten Mile Range. Indeed, my little cane was of so much service to me that I came to look upon it as a personal friend that cared almost as much for me as I did for it. It pushed aside thorny bushes and nettlesome weeds when I was looking for nests, thus saving my hands many a painful wound. And more than one serpent, including the rattlesnake, has had his head crushed or his spine broken by sturdy blows from my little wild-cherry cane. I should add that it had a hooked handle, so that I could hang it on the strap of my haversack when I needed both hands.

In the beginning of your observations you will find the work of identifying the birds a rare and exciting pleasure; then, after you have named all the species in your neighborhood, it will be no less delightful to study their interesting ways, or to extend your researches to other fields. And if at any time you observe some odd bits of bird behavior which you think will be news to the many bird lovers the world over, why should you not report them to one of the bird magazines, so that others may share the pleasures of your discoveries? An admirer of feathered folk should not be selfish; indeed, I do not see how he can be.

It simply remains to be said that this volume is an illustration of the method of bird study just indicated. In the first place, I shall show, in a few chapters, how the student goes about his work of identifying species and making new bird friends; then will follow a number of monographs indicating how much may be learned about the life histories of several interesting species; next there will be a miscellaneous collection of incidents of bird life, showing how many odds and ends the industrious and observing rambler may gather by the way; and, finally, the book will conclude with four somewhat technical chapters on bird education, bird music, bird flight, and bird feet, which I hope will prove interesting as well as instructive.

MAKING NEW FRIENDS

A friend once told me of a letter he had received from a correspondent who is an enthusiastic botanist. The writer, having just returned from an excursion in which he found a flower that was new to him, gave vent to his feelings of exultation by exclaiming, "Oh, the joy! the joy!" A like experience comes to the bird lover when he makes a new acquaintance in the feathered domain, no matter how many other observers may have seen and studied the species. "A bird that is new to me is to all intents and purposes a new bird," is his self-complacent mode of reasoning, though it may not be distinguished for its logic.

Chipping Sparrow

After studying the birds in Ohio and Indiana for a good many years, I moved to eastern Kansas, where I lived for five and a half years. My rambles were by no means confined to the wooded bluffs and hollows that bound the Missouri River on the west, for I also made excursions out upon the prairies of Kansas, over into the state of Missouri, and down into Oklahoma; and everywhere I carried my field glass with me and kept both eyes intent on the birds. You would expect an enthusiast in the pursuit of bird lore to do nothing else. What a pleasure it was to ramble about in new fields and make acquaintance with new bird friends! There is not a very marked difference between the avifauna of eastern Kansas and Ohio, and yet there are some birds found in the former state that are not met with in the latter--enough to keep the observer on the tiptoe of expectancy for several months.

One of my new acquaintances was a little bird which is known as the clay-colored sparrow. It belongs to the same genus (Spizella) as the chipping and field sparrows which are so well known in the East; but it has an individuality of its own, and is not merely a copy. I stumbled upon it while pursuing my explorations near Peabody, far out on the level prairie, where the species was abundant during the season of migration. As I was sauntering along a road, a peculiar croaking little trill greeted me from the hedge, sounding very much like the rasping call of certain kinds of grasshoppers when they are suddenly startled and take to wing. But no insect had ever emitted quite such a sound in my hearing. This could not be an insect. It was worth while to look and make sure of the identity of the odd musician.

After some difficulty, I fixed my glass upon a number of little sparrows about the size of the chippies. They bore a close resemblance to that species too, save that the crown-piece and the general tone of the back were decidedly darker, while the under parts were a good deal whiter. The clear, ash-colored cervical interval between the crown and the back and the distinct brown loral and auricular space told me plainly who the little charmers were. Not at the moment, however, for the birds were new to me, and I had to wait until I could consult my manual before I was able to decide that they were the clay-colored sparrows.

Their song is an odd vocal performance--a low, croaking trill, preceded by a few longer notes, all delivered in the same key. It is, in fact, a contralto solo divided into brief stanzas, and easily might be mistaken for the grating buzz of an insect, especially if heard at a distance of a few rods. It possesses little or no musical quality, and is perhaps the most curious style of bird minstrelsy with which I am acquainted. In comparison the chippie's trill sounds loud and clear and bell-like, with a distinctly melodious quality of tone. The song of the little clay-colored sparrow is also marked by a kind of drawl, giving one the impression that the bird is just a little too lazy to exert himself; yet when you get him in the field of your glass and see him throw back his head, expand his throat and chest, and open his mandibles as wide as he can, you quickly decide that he is not the apathetic creature his desultory song would lead you to infer. It really is laughable, and almost pathetic, too, to note how much energy he expends in the production of his poor little aria.

Indeed, not in the least sluggish is the blood flowing in the veins of Spizella pallida, for he is a vivacious little body, flitting about actively in the hedges and bushes, and sometimes mounting into the trees, chanting his little alto strain all the while, as if his life depended upon it. He is one of the comparatively few birds who is lavish of his song in migration.

Unlike the familiar chippie, he does not usually find a perch in plain sight, from which to rehearse his song, but keeps himself well hidden in the bushes or trees, darting into a hiding place as soon as he thinks himself discovered. The shy little imp prefers to put a screen of foliage or twigs between himself and the observer. Might his motto be, "Little birds should be heard and not seen"? I had quite a time making sure of him, but, as a pleasant compensation, when his identity was once settled, I could not well have mistaken him for another species, for he is a bird of real distinction.

My study of the clay-colored sparrows was restricted to their habits in migration, at which time they move about in more or less compact little flocks, gathering seeds and chanting their monotonous trills. While I first found these sparrows near Peabody, they were also fairly common, a few days later, in northeastern Kansas, about a mile back from the Missouri River, where their low alto strains formed a kind of gray background for the high-pitched trills of the Harris sparrows and the loud pipings of the cardinals. Quaint as our little contralto's solos are, they have a distinct fascination for me, and now that I no longer live in the Sunflower state, I miss them sorely when the springtime comes.

These sparrows do not, I believe, breed in Kansas, but are known to establish their households in the northern part of Illinois, central and northern Iowa, the Red River region in Minnesota, the country drained by the upper Missouri River and its tributaries, Manitoba as far north as the Saskatchewan River, and the plains and bases of the foothills of eastern Colorado. Their nests are built on the ground or in low bushes, and from three to five eggs, of a greenish-blue tint, flecked with cinnamon-brown, are deposited. They spend the winters in southern Texas and still farther south. Only "accidentally," as the word goes, are they known in the eastern part of the United States, and for that reason little has yet been written about them in popular books on birds. The time will come, no doubt, when they will have a well-recognized place in bird literature, just as the chippie, the vesper sparrow, and the song sparrow have to-day.

In bird study it is never safe to take too much for granted. One must be constantly on the alert, and, more than that, one must be able to make fine distinctions with both the ear and the eye. Here is a case in point. For many days, while strolling about in quest of bird lore, I heard a quaint little song in the bushy clumps, and that, too, in some of the most out-of-the-way places. "It is nothing but the house wren," I muttered to myself, I know not how often. "It isn't worth while to look for it when there are new birds to be found. Still, it's singular," I continued, "that the house wren should dwell in such secluded places. It would seem that his name is a misnomer--at least, in a good many instances." Several times I stopped to listen more intently to the rolling ditty. "There's something odd about that wren's song," I repeated. "Does the house wren always close its song with the rising inflection, as if it were asking a question?"

Then I would perhaps make a half-hearted attempt to get a glimpse of the lyrist, but it kept itself well hidden in the bushes, and I desisted, begrudging the time taken from my quest for feathered rarities. But one day, while strolling along the banks of a small stream, I again heard the labored ditty, and the next moment a small bird darted into full view, calling and scolding in an agitated way, and, while I watched it capering about, it broke into the very song to which for several weeks I had been listening so carelessly. Why, it was not a wren after all! It did not look like a wren, nor act like one, but, rather, its form and conduct were like those of a vireo; and a vireo it was. My bird manual soon settled that point. And what was the name of the little stranger who had introduced himself in so informal a way? It was the Bell vireo, an entirely new species to me.

It is not an eastern species; it ranges from Illinois to the base of the Rocky Mountains. In Kansas it is a summer resident, hanging its little basket of a nest on the twigs of bushes or low trees, after the regular vireo fashion. It was my good fortune to find a nest on a copsy hilltop, where the bird's madrigals and lullabies mingled with those of the yellow-breasted chats, the indigo buntings, the blue-gray gnat catchers, and the Kentucky warblers. To this day I feel a longing to visit the secluded spot where I held so many pleasant interviews with these birds.

Another Kansas bird that was new to my eyes and that afforded me much delight was the Harris sparrow--a distinctively western species, not known, or at least very rarely, east of the Mississippi River. He is truly a fine bird, a little larger than the fox sparrow, neatly clad, his breast prettily decorated with a brooch of black spots held in place by a slender necklace of the same color, while his throat and forehead are bordered with black. His rump and upper tail coverts are a delicate shade of grayish brown, by which he may be readily distinguished from the fox sparrow, whose rear parts are reddish brown. His beak, feet, and legs are of a pinkish tint, making him look quite trig and dressy. The latest of the spring arrivals were the most highly colored, having the whole chin, throat, and top of the head a glossy, uniform black.

It would appear that the most matured individuals migrate farthest south in winter. That, at least, would be the natural conclusion, judging from the fact that they arrive latest in the spring in our central latitudes. In the southern part of Kansas the Harris sparrows are said to be common winter sojourners, but in the north-eastern part of the state they disappeared in November or December, and did not return until the middle of February, or later if the weather happened to be severe. From the time of their vernal arrival they were to be seen in every ramble until they took flight for their breeding haunts in the North. One spring some of them were still loitering in Kansas on the eleventh of May, and were singing blithely, no doubt waiting for the winter cold of their summer homes to be well past before they ventured farther toward the arctic lands.

In general, the habits of these birds are much like those of the white-throated sparrows, which are much more common in the East than in the West. The Harris sparrows are fond of copses and hedges, and especially of brush heaps in new grounds. So marked, indeed, is their penchant for brush heaps that I almost wish one might re-christen them "brush-heap sparrows." Many a time I have played a little trick on the unsuspecting birds by stealing up to a brush pile and giving it a sudden blow with my cane; then a whole covey of them would dash pellmell from their covert with loud chirps of protest against such wantonness.

Sometimes they are found in the depths of the woods, providing there is thick underbrush in which they can conceal themselves. I seldom found them in open places either in the woods or fields. Yet, shy as they are, they have a fondness for the dense hedges along the highways, flitting and chirping as the traveler passes by.

Being wary birds, they do not wander far from their hiding places, into which they precipitate themselves at the approach of a supposed danger. It was quite a while before I could get a clear view of their breasts, for, with provoking persistence, they kept their tails turned toward me. However, when once you really become acquainted with a bird, it seems to lose part of its shyness, and so after a time I often had the Harris sparrows in plain view. One of their characteristic habits was to stand at full height on the top of a brush heap, with tail lifted, crest feathers erect, and eyes wide open, the picture of wild alertness. In such poses they are indeed handsome birds.

It was March 5, 1898, when I heard the first song of this sparrow, and even then it was only a fragment of a song. But, the weather remaining pleasant, the sixteenth of the month brought a fine concert. The bird's song was a surprise to me. It began with a prolonged run so much like the opening tremolo of the white-throated sparrow that it might have led the most expert ornithologist astray. The fact is, I looked around for quite a while in search of a white-throat, thinking him still a little out of tune, and therefore unable to finish his chanson; and I was undeceived only by the singing of several Harris sparrows that with unusual boldness had perched in plain sight. The resemblance ceased, however, with the opening notes, for the western bird did not add the sweet, rhythmic triad of his white-throated cousin, the closing part of his song being only a somewhat labored trill of no distinct character, and not fulfilling the promise of his initial strain.

In the concerts of these birds--and frequently many of them would be trilling at the same time--they sang in several different keys, some of them striking the treble and others dropping almost to the alto. Occasionally two birds in different parts of a field would sing responsively, one trill running very high in the scale, the other an octave lower. It seemed almost as if the responsive exercise was engaged in intentionally.

The Harris sparrow has another song which is quite unlike his melodious trill. It is delivered in a loud voice of little musical quality, and the notes are pounded out in a percussive style, like the explosion in quick succession of a number of little cartridges. Yet you must be quite close to the bird in order to hear the queer canticle distinctly, and when you do hear it you will wonder why nature ever put such a song into a bird's larynx. The Harris sparrow also utters an explosive alarm-call, which expresses not a little petulance and concern.

One day a pretty picture was made by two of these birds that stood face to face on a brush heap, bowing at each other, each threatening to peck the other's head off, and both singing all the while at the top of their voices, yet each afraid, in spite of his bluster, to close with his opponent in actual contest. It was a miniature exhibition of the beak-to-beak challenging often indulged in by two rival cocks of the farmyard. For some minutes the little farce was kept up, then one of the birds became tired of the game and darted over to the next brush heap.

I have said that these birds are scarcely known east of the Mississippi River, but Mr. Ridgway says that they are occasionally seen during migration in Illinois and Wisconsin. In eastern Kansas and western Missouri they are common, almost abundant, during both the vernal and autumnal migrations, and after you have once cultivated their acquaintance they are likable, if not quite companionable, birds. But familiar as they are in the regions named, they are still something of a mystery to the naturalists of our country, for Mr. Ridgway says that their "breeding range is unknown," save that there is a doubtful record of one nest at Fort Custer, Montana; while Mrs. Bailey says: "The breeding range of the Harris sparrow is unknown except for Mr. Preble's Fort Churchill record. The last of July, among the dwarf spruces of Fort Churchill, he found an adult male and female with young just from the nest." It will be remembered that Fort Churchill is away up on the coast of the Hudson Bay. It is probable, therefore, that the nest of the Harris sparrow has never been found by any of the naturalists of America. Who would suppose that these birds, so numerous and so well known in Kansas, would, in the breeding season, surround themselves with such an air of mystery?

It was in Kansas, too, that I really came to know the Lincoln sparrow and hear his song, although I had caught a few fleeting glimpses of him in the East, and also in the neighborhood of Duluth, Minnesota. In the Sunflower state his conduct was just about as inconsistent as it could have been without being downright absurd. What do I mean by that? Why, while he was as wild as a deer, he still came to town, flitting about in the bushes of a vacant lot near my house, and even visiting the fence between my yard and the adjoining one, hopping about on the ground with one eye on the lookout for nits and worms and the other for human disturbers. My attention was first drawn to him by hearing a squeaky little trill in the vacant lot. But, my! how wary he was when I went out to find him! The song bore some resemblance to that of the house wren, but had not so rolling and gurgling a quality, and was pitched to a slightly higher and finer key. For a long time he kept himself ensconced in the thicket, trilling saucily at intervals, as if daring me to find him if I could, and when I finally drove him out of his hiding place, he darted off in a zigzag course to another bush clump, into which he dropped in the greatest possible haste.

By and by his curiosity got the better of him, and he flitted to the top of a brush heap and peeped out at me surreptitiously. My glass was upon him in a moment, revealing his whitish throat and mottled chest washed with buff, the latter being his characteristic marking. A few days later he was singing in a small apple tree by my neighbor's fence. I stole as close to him as I could and peered at him through my binocular, while he returned the compliment by peering at me, and then warily ventured to rehearse his little tune. The least movement on my part would startle him, cause him to flit to another perch and crane out his neck to glare at me questioningly with wild, dilated eyes, uncertain whether I was to be trusted or not. Both of us presently grew tired of our strained position, and so I walked off and he flew away. No doubt there was mutual satisfaction in the inspection we gave each other; at least, I felt well satisfied with having heard the song of so shy a bird. His stay in my neighborhood lasted only a few days; then he left as mysteriously as he had come, without even the courtesy of a good-bye. He went to his summer home in the North, and I did not see him again until the next spring, just twelve months later almost to the day.

WILDWOOD MINSTRELS*

* Parts of this and several other chapters of this book were first published in The New York Times, whose courtesy in permitting him to reprint, the author hereby acknowledges.

Nothing affords the bird student more pleasure than settling the identity of species, albeit sometimes it is hard and patience-trying work. And of all the birds, none are so provokingly and charmingly elusive as some of the wood warblers. What a time I had for several years in making sure of some of these little nymph-like creatures which were flitting about in the foliage of the trees, concealing themselves by a leafy barrier! Many a weary chase did they lead me through the woods, and more than once I almost unjointed my neck by long-continued looking up.

For identifying the tree-top flitters an opera glass is scarcely powerful enough. A field glass or a Bausch & Lomb binocular is really a necessity. It draws the bird right down to you, while at the same time the elusive creature remains at what it regards a safe distance. Its conduct will therefore not be constrained, and the observer can study it in its natural poses.

What an enigma the Tennessee warbler for a long time remained to me! Never still for a moment, yet so indistinctly marked that at a distance it looks like a dozen other birds one might name—a veritable feathered rebus. But finally I fixed its place in the avian schedule with the help of my field glass—white under parts, slightly tinged with yellow, back and rump olive green, top and sides of head delicate bluish-ash; no eye-ring, no wing-bars. There is no other warbler marked quite like that. And yet its song is its most conspicuous mark, so to speak, for it is a loud, shrill, and very rapidly repeated run, which might be spelled out in this way: "Chippy, chippy, chippy, chippity-chippity-chippity." The whole song is emitted at a galloping pace, giving you the impression that the bird is in a desperate hurry. Important business on hand, no doubt! Yes, there is a worm or a nit on the under side of that leaf, and he must nab it now or never! With such pressing business matters on hand, he has no time for regaling you with "linked sweetness long drawn out."

Still, he sometimes does prolong his ditty, giving it a saucy, challenging air. No other warbler sings so loudly. His voice is as shrill and penetrating as that of the indigo bird, though the song is quite different in technique.

[Illustration: Yellow Warbler]

Another feathered conundrum was the Nashville warbler, whose back and head are colored like those of the Tennessee, but whose under parts are bright yellow, instead of white or white only slightly washed with yellow; and, besides, sharp peering through your glass will reveal a distinct white ring encircling the eye. The bird in the hand would also show a dainty chestnut patch on the crown, but this mark is seldom seen while it is flitting about in the leafy trees. The songs of the Nashville and the Tennessee are somewhat similar, but not the same, the Tennessee's being louder, shriller, and more sharply accentuated, while his cousin's is more liquid and musical and far less sibilant. My notes represent the Nashville's song phonetically as follows: "Swee, swee, swee, ah-wit-ah-wit-ah-wit," delivered rapidly in a high key and with not a little energy and emphasis. When my notes were made the little lyrist was putting his best foot forward, and was not high in the trees, so that I heard him distinctly. The Tennessee warblers were also singing near at hand, giving me a good opportunity to compare the arias of the two species.

Belonging to the same subfamily is the orange-crowned warbler. It has not so marked a preference for trees as its little relatives just mentioned, but likes, so far as my observation goes, to flit about in thickets, where it remains in hiding until driven from its covert or drawn forth by curiosity. Only for a moment does it appear in sight, then plunges into another covert. You will note that its eye-ring is yellow, and that its under parts are neither bright yellow, like the Nashville's, nor white, like the Tennessee's, but greenish yellow obscurely streaked on the chest. I have never heard the song of the orange-crown.

There are a number of shy warblers that are especially partial to wild, unfrequented parts of the woods, where they are seldom disturbed by human intruders. In Kansas I found them in the deep, densely wooded ravines running back from the Missouri River and its tributary valleys. Although these feathered recluses are rarely molested by man, they seem to know enough about his character to look upon him with a suspicious eye when he ventures into their sylvan domain. Hence they are hard to study, and it is not often that their deftly hidden nests can be found.

One of the most delightful of these hermits is the Kentucky warbler. A brilliant little bird he is, with his golden under parts and superciliary line, his black patch on the cheek just below the eye, his black cap, and his coat of iridescent olive green. You will not mistake him for the Maryland yellow-throat, which also wears a black patch on the side of his head; but this patch lies over the eye and includes it, and its upper border is white, while this bird lacks the yellow and curved superciliary band. Besides, the yellow-throat is not a woodland but a marsh bird. The Kentucky warbler is attractive in many ways. An industrious minstrel, his voice is strong and full for so small a bird, and until you learn to know his tune well, you may mistake it for that of the cardinal. But, as a piper, he lacks the versatility of the cardinal, who carries a number of music sheets in his repertory, while the little Kentuckian confines his lyrical efforts principally to one strain. Sometimes he delivers his intermittent aria from a low bush or even from the ground, but his favorite song-perches are the branches of saplings and trees just below the zone of foliage. Here, in the shadows, you may be compelled to look for him for some time before you espy his trig little form, and even then you are likely to see him because he flits to another perch rather than because you first catch the glint of his colors. Whether he means it or not, he is something of a ventriloquist, for which reason you will often look for him in many places before seeing him.

As I have noted, he is an untiring singer. It never occurred to me to time him, but Dr. Frank M. Chapman has had the patience to do so. "On one occasion," says this observer, "at Englewood, New Jersey, I watched a male for three hours. During this period, with the exception of five interruptions of less than forty-five seconds each, he sang with the greatest regularity once every twelve seconds. Thus, allowing for the brief intervals of silence, he sang about 875 times, or some 5,250 notes. I found him singing, and when I departed he showed no signs of ceasing." It is such painstaking observations that add something new and fresh to our knowledge of birds.

The Kentucky warbler is fond of walking about on the ground in the woods, seeking for his favorite insects. As you slowly follow, you will now and then catch a glimpse of him through the apertures of the leaves; then he will again disappear beneath his canvas of green. Thus he pursues his quest hour after hour, and you may hear the rustle of his tiny feet upon the carpet of dead leaves. Is it only a notion of mine, or am I correct, in thinking that his promenades on the ground are mostly taken early in the spring before there is danger from snakes?

I like the pretty Kentuckians, but must grant you that in some respects they are quite exasperating, never inclined to be as confiding as some other birds. And then most birds will sooner or later betray the presence of their nests, but the Kentucky warblers seldom do so, knowing too well how to keep their procreant secrets. They have evidently learned the use of strategy, as you will see: One day a pair began to chirp vigorously as I approached their demesne in a lonely hollow, and I felt a thrill of joy at the prospect of finding a nest. One of them even flitted about with a worm in its bill--a sure sign of nestlings in the neighborhood. For nearly four hours I watched the chirping couple, and peered, as I thought, into every nook and cranny of the place, but all in vain; neither nest nor bantlings could I find. Yet in some way that seemed almost mysterious enough to be uncanny, the mother bird got rid of the tidbit which she held in her bill. She probably decided to eat it herself rather than betray the whereabouts of her younglings. I have seen more than one parent bird do that.

A few days later, in the same hollow, a Kentucky warbler was singing contentedly, showing no signs of uneasiness. The female was not to be seen or heard. I stalked about a long time, hoping to flush her from her nest, but all my efforts were as futile that day as they had been on my previous visit. In another hollow, on the same day, I watched a Kentucky warbler flitting about with a worm in her bill. Again and again she disappeared somewhere in the tanglewood, and came back with an empty bill to chirp her disapproval of my spying; but look as I would in the very places where she went down, I could discover no nest. In Warbledom it is evidently no violation of ethical principles to act a lie in order to protect a nestful of bantlings.

But my story is not to have a disappointing ending, after all, for in the spring and summer of 1902 my stars became auspicious, and I found three Kentucky warblers' nests that were tenanted and several more that were already deserted. Perhaps the turning of my luck was due not so much to accident as to the fact that I had "caught on," and knew more about their ruses. One of the nests discovered is worth describing.

It was on a hilltop in Kansas, blown by the freshest breezes that sweep over the limitless prairies. An ideal spot, indeed, for the nesting of birds that love lone places. In one of my rambles I found this pleasant elevation, and was attracted by the possibilities it offered for bird study. Presently a male Kentucky warbler appeared with a couple of large worms in his beak, and I made up my mind to find his nest if perseverance could accomplish that object. So I sat down in the shade of a tree and watched the bird closely. Now note his admirable finesse. After flitting about among the bushes for a minute or two, chirping his protest at my presence, he descended into the copse below and disappeared. Of course, any student of birds would have supposed that he had gone down near the nest to feed his bairns, and that he only needed to go and examine the place to discover the little avian secret. My pulses thrilled more than a little as I began my search for the nest right where the bird had descended into the thicket. But do you know that my most strenuous efforts--and they were strenuous on a hot day like that--resulted only in disappointment? The nest was not to be found within a radius of a rod from the point where the little diplomat went down. A few days later I made my way to the hilltop, and do you know that the shrewd bird played me the same trick? He scuttled down into the bushes at almost the same point as before, and no nest rewarded my search. I went home just about ready to give up my search for Kentucky warblers' nests, for I had been hunting them for a number of years without success.

However, in a few days I found my way again to the breezy hilltop. The chats, vireos, and indigo birds gave due warning of my approach, and I felt sure that Master Kentucky and his mate would be on their guard. To my delight, in a few minutes the female presented herself in one of the trees, her bill holding a bunch of worms.

Luckily she was not so wary or diplomatic as her husband, and, in addition, she extremely anxious to feed her hungry babies. Instead of going over to the copse where the male bird had played me such a clever trick, she flew down the path about four rods to a small scrub oak, from which she soon dropped into the weeds below. Then I said to myself; "Aha!" and smiled in a knowing way.

I walked down the path to the tree, but no Kentucky warblers were to be seen--not right away. So I sat down in the path and waited to see what would happen. It was only a short time till the female appeared, with a telltale bunch of worms in her beak. A moment later her mate also arrived, carrying a small worm in the usual way. The situation was growing interesting. The two birdlets chirped and flitted about in the tree for a long time, afraid to go down to the nest. I moved slowly and cautiously farther up the path to give them a better chance to divulge their secret. Presently the pretty madame summoned courage to drop to a lower perch in the tree, then to a still lower one, then to the top of one of the bushes below, and at last into the weed clump and out of sight.

I wasted no time. In a minute I was pressing the weeds apart and looking down admiringly into the little cot with its four half-fledged occupants--the first Kentucky warbler's nest I had ever seen. Set upon the ground, its bulky foundation of dry leaves supported the cup proper, which was lined with fine grass. Easy enough to find when you knew precisely where to look for it.

Think now of the little game the male bird had played me on my previous visits to the haunt! He had descended into the copse about four rods distant from the nest instead of going down near its site; then he had doubtless followed a secret pathway through the weeds and bushes to the nest, fed his children, and hurried away without letting himself be seen.

The parent birds did not like the idea of my finding and inspecting their nest, for they chirped and darted about in a panic. To relieve their anguish I retired up the slope a short distance, seated myself in the pleasant shade of a scrub oak, and made an entry of my find in my notebook. Alas! I had probably done harm to my little friends without intending it, for their chirping attracted the attention of one of their worst foes, and drew him to the spot. I loitered about for perhaps ten minutes, and then decided to take one more peep at the pretty domicile before leaving the hilltop. As I drew near, I observed that the parent birds were chirping in a low, but heart-broken way, as if they were almost stricken dumb with terror. Were they so badly frightened because I was returning to their nest?

I stepped up cautiously and looked down at the nest. It was now my turn to give vent to a cry of consternation, for what I saw was this: A large blacksnake coiled about the nest, the fold of his neck wabbling to and fro in a terrifying way, while with his mouth he was trying to seize one of the bantlings. Fortunately I had a good-sized stick, almost a club, in my hand, and I wasted no time in bringing it down with all the force I could command upon the serpent, taking care to deliver the blow at the side of the nest. The snake tried to uncoil, but another blow broke his backbone, if indeed the first one had not done so, and he was in my power. He had swallowed one of the nestlings, but three were left, and seemed to be in good condition. On my return to the place a few days later the nest was empty, and I fear that the remaining little ones had also been destroyed, perhaps by the mate of the snake from which I had rescued them.

On the shelf of a steep bluff covered with a riot of bushes and briars a pair of hooded warblers found a dwelling place to their taste in the spring of 1900. This handsome birdlet may be known by his dainty yellow hood, bordered with black, and cannot be mistaken for any other member of the great feathered fraternity. One cannot look at him without feeling that Nature tried to see what she could do in the way of an unusual arrangement of colors. Who can tell what impelled her to make a living gem like this, as odd as it is beautiful?

On the side of the bluff referred to I was first attracted by the vivacious song of the little male, which I had not heard for several years--not since an excursion I had taken into Louisiana and Mississippi. His voice was clear and ringing, and the tune he executed was by no means a meager performance.

One day a loud, metallic chirping was heard, and presently two hooded warblers appeared, each with the proverbial green worm in its beak. I decided to remain in the nook and watch, for the nesting habits of these rare warblers were new to me. In and out, up and down, here and there, they flitted, making a checker-work of black and gold amid the foliage, craning their necks, peering at me with anxious inquiry in their dark little eyes, and filling the woodland with their uneasy chirping.

It was a long time to wait, but at length patience had its reward; one of the birds flew down to the bushes on the steep slope above me and fed a youngster in plain view. No time was lost in pushing through the bushy tangle to the magic spot. Behold! it was a young cowbird that had been fed by the devoted little mother! That was trying beyond expression--to think that all the efforts of the pretty couple, all their intense solicitude, was wasted on a great, hulking impostor like the cowbird. He had just scrambled from the nest, from which he had doubtless previously crowded the rightful heirs of the family to perish from starvation on the ground. I found the nest only about a foot away from the perch of the young bird--a deep, neat little basket, compactly felted with down and plant fibers, set in the crotch of a slender bush of the thicket. It was certainly too small to accommodate any tenants besides the strapping young cowbird. In the spring of 1902 another hooded warbler's nest rewarded my search. Its holdings were four callow bantlings, all of which were carried off by some marauder before my next visit.

Another little charmer of the woodland, especially of thick second-growth timber, is the blue-winged warbler, which glories in the high-sounding Latin name of Helminthophila pinus. Wherever seen, he would attract attention on account of the peculiar cut and color of his clothes. A conspicuous black line reaching from the corner of the mouth back through the eye is a diagnostic feature of his plumage, while his crown and breast gleam in bright yellow, almost golden in the sunshine; his wings and tail are blue-gray, with some white trimmings, and his back and rump are bright olive There you have an array of colors that makes a picture indeed. Madame Blue-wing wears the same pattern as her lord, but the hues are less brilliant.

The manners of Sir Blue-wing--I call him so because of his distinguished air--are interesting, for they differ, in one respect at least, from those of most of the other warblers of my acquaintance. He flits about among the branches in rather a leisurely way--for a warbler; but his main characteristic is his unwarbler-like fashion of clinging back downward to the under side of the twigs, after the manner of the chickadee, in order to secure the nits and worms under the leaves. He acts decidedly like a diminutive trapeze performer.

His song consists of an insect-like buzz, divided into stanzas of two syllables each, with a pensive strain running through it, as if the heart of the little singer were filled with sadness. While it sounds rather faint at a distance, close at hand it has a strangely penetrating quality.

Although my numerous efforts to find a blue-wing's nest were unavailing, I had the satisfaction of proving beyond doubt that these birds breed in northeastern Kansas. A quaint, squeaking call attracted my attention one day, and I found that it proceeded from the throat of a young blue-wing perched in the bushes, for presently the mamma came and thrust a morsel into the open mouth of the bantling. Some young birds sit quietly and patiently, waiting for their rations, and utter only a faint twitter when they are fed; but the youthful blue-wings are not of so contented and silent a disposition. On the contrary, they are noisy little fellows, making their presence known to friend and foe alike, although they are very careful never to permit the human observer to come too close. They are duly warned of danger by their ever-vigilant parents. Sometimes a youngster will sit on the same perch for a long time, preening his feathers and uttering a little call at intervals, just to keep in practice, as it were; while at other times he will pursue his parents about in the woods, loudly demanding his dinner. One season I succeeded in finding at least five pairs of these warblers, in company with their clamorous broods. The nest is set on the ground in the bushes and grass of second-growth timber tracts. Lined with tendrils and fine strips of bark, it is "firmly wrapped with numerous leaves, whose stems point upward." Another haunter of the dusky depths of the woods is the ovenbird. His song is one of the most peculiar in warblerdom. Beginning in moderate tones, it grows louder and louder as it nears the end, and really seems like a voice moving toward you. This bird also walks about in the woods, and does not hop, as most of his relatives do. As he walks about on his leafy carpet, his head erect, he has quite a consequential air. He derives his name from the fact that his nest, set on the ground, is globular in form, with the entrance at one side, giving it the appearance of a small oven.

The gay redstarts, which seem to be so tame and confiding in the early spring, turn into veritable eremites in the breeding season, seeking the most secluded portions of the woods as their habitat. Their little nests are harder to find than one would suppose; yet I have had the good fortune to watch two females erecting the walls of their tiny cottages, and a pretty sight it was.

The redstart has some interesting ways. One of them is his habit of spreading out his wings and tail as he perches or flits about in the trees, as if he were anxious to display the fiery trimmings that so elegantly set off his little black suit. Blood will tell, for I have seen the young redstarts imitating their parents by spreading out their odd, croppy tails in a comical way.

How early in life young birds are taught some of the lessons that are needful for their own safety! One day I heard a young redstart chirping for his dinner. I quietly thrust my head into the thicket, and soon espied the birdkin perched on a twig only about a rod away. He either did not see me, or else decided that I was not a bugaboo. A few minutes later the mother darted into the enclosure and fed her baby. She was too much absorbed in her duties to notice me until the repast was over; then she suddenly caught sight of her unwelcome caller. She stood transfixed with astonishment for one breathless moment, then uttered a piercing cry of alarm that sent the little one dashing away like a streak of lightning. Plainly the youngster understood his mamma's signal, for until she uttered it he had sat perfectly quiet and unconcerned, perhaps not even aware of my presence. Birds are taught the language of fear at a tender age. Of course they learn it so readily because there is a basis of timidity in their natures, implanted by heredity.

CHICKADEE WAYS*

*Reprinted by permission, from "Our Animal Friends," New York.

Blank-capped Chickadee

In a somewhat casual way, and without going into their natural history, the last two chapters have indicated the method of making an acquaintance with new species and of studying the habits of a few wild birds. A few chapters will now be devoted to a fuller study of a number of interesting birds. Not that I expect to write their complete life histories, which, indeed, would not be necessary; but that I may give you some idea of the large amount of knowledge that can be gained of one species. If this were multiplied by the knowledge procurable from the study of all the members of the feathered brotherhood, think what an education the whole would give one. Let us begin with the familiar little tomtit.

In his valuable manual, "Birds of Eastern North America," Dr. Frank M. Chapman calls the little black-capped chickadee an "animated bunch of black and white feathers." That is certainly a graphic and correct way of putting it, for no bird is more active and alert than this little major with the black skull cap and ashy-blue coat. Everybody knows him, I take it, but if any more points are needed for his identification, you must look for a little bird which, in addition to his cap of glossy black, wears a bib of the same color, buckled up close to his chin, with a wedge of white inserted on each side of his neck between the black of his throat and crown to the corner of his mouth.

If all birds were as sociably disposed as the little tomtit--for that is also one of his names--bird study would be a delight, and almost a sinecure. Trustful and fearless, he often comes within a few feet of you, and fixes you with his keen little eyes, which dart out innumerable interrogation points. Sometimes he calls his own name in a saucy way, "Chick-a-dee-dee, chick-a-dee-dee," which, being interpreted, means, "What is your business here, sir? Aren't you out of your proper latitude?" Occasionally he will grow terribly excited over your presence--or at least pretend to-- scolding and shaming you until you feel yourself a real interloper; at other times he will salute you in the most affable way, as if bidding you welcome to his haunts and inviting you to come often and make yourself at home. What a pity it is he cannot talk, and let us know what he really thinks of us and of the world in general! Dr. Chapman says that on two occasions chickadees have flown down and perched on his hand, giving him the feeling that he was being taken into their confidence.

Watch Master Tomtit as he performs some of his acrobatic feats, putting the tilters and tumblers in the human circus to the blush. He often hangs back downward from a slender twig or even a leaf, and daintily picks the nits that have ensconced themselves in the buds or foliage. Let his flexile perch sway in the wind as it will, he is safe, for if the twig should break or his hold should slip, which seldom occurs, he can recover himself at once by spreading his nimble wings, wheeling about, and alighting on a perch below. Ah, yes! the tomtit is the embodiment and poetry of nimbleness.

But he is more than a mere feathered gentleman; he is an extremely useful citizen. Prof. E. D. Sanderson published a valuable article in "The Auk" for April 1898, in which he proved that this bird serves a most useful purpose as an insecticide. He examined the craws of twenty-eight chickadees, nineteen of them secured in the winter and nine in the spring. During the winter 70.7 per cent of the food found in these stomachs was animal, while in the spring no vegetable matter was found at all, the birds subsisting entirely on insects and their eggs and larvae. By far the larger part of the insects thus destroyed were of the noxious species that bore into the bark and wood of the trees or sting the fruit. An orchard in which several chickadees had taken up their abode one winter and spring was so well cleared of canker worms that an excellent yield of fruit was grown, whereas the trees of other orchards in the neighborhood were largely defoliated by the destructive worms, and there was no yield of fruit.

Professor Sanderson made an interesting estimate of the economic value of our little scavengers. In the state of Michigan, where his observations were made, he thinks that a fair average is seven chickadees to the square mile. If each bird should destroy fifty-five insects per day, which is a very modest estimate, the seven birds would consume three hundred and eighty-five every day, making about 137,500 per year in each square mile. In this way about eight billions of insects would be destroyed annually in the state--an economic fact whose importance cannot be overestimated.

The same investigator also thinks that it would be wise for farmers and fruit-growers to encourage the chickadees to make their homes in orchards, and this could be done, he says, "by placing food for them till they feel at home, by erecting suitable nesting sites, and by careful protection"; to which I would add, by leaving a few old snags in the trees where the birds can find natural nesting places. Besides the useful purpose the birds would serve, what pleasant companions they would be, piping, both summer and winter, their sweet minor tunes!

No one can deny that the tomtit is a companionable little fellow. In addition to his vigorous call of "Chick-a-dee-dee," he whistles, as has been said, a sweet minor strain which may be represented by the syllables, "Phe-e-be-e," repeated again and again. Often in midwinter, when bland days come, and even in very cold weather, too, sometimes, he will pipe his pensive air, which floats through the woods like a song of chastened sadness.

Not infrequently two tits will engage in what may be called a "responsive exercise," swinging their two-part song back and forth in the woods like a silvery pendulum. Not soon shall I forget a winter day on which I listened with delight to such an antiphonal duet. I was standing in a road that wound along the foot of a steep, wooded bluff, and the two minstrels were in the woods above me, one of them singing very high in the scale, the other responding in the same tune, but almost, if not quite, an octave lower. At first they were about twenty rods apart, but as they swung back and forth, they gradually approached each other until the distance between them was only a few feet. The music seemed like a slender thread of silver which was being wound up at both ends, gradually drawing the little fluters together. Sometimes one of them would miss one note of his dissyllabic song, and at times the refrains were repeated in a leisurely way, at times in quick succession; but the performers never sang simultaneously, each waiting until his fellow minstrel had given his reply. The pleasing duet lasted for many minutes; indeed, it was kept up long after I left the immediate neighborhood, for when I had gone quite a distance the sweet cadenzas still fell rhythmically on my ear. To my mind the two-part aria seemed like a voluntary performance, and I cannot doubt that it was. There was too much of an air of purpose about it to permit of the thought that it was a mere accident or coincidence; but whether it was a musical contest between rival vocalists, or the love song of a tomtit and his mate, I could not determine.

Cunning in other ways, it would be strange if the tomtits did not display acuteness in the selection of nesting sites. A cosy hollow in a dead snag or stump is especially acceptable. Sometimes it is a deserted woodpecker's cavity made trig and clean, while quite often, when the wood is soft enough, the tits themselves chisel out a little hole in a tree or stump or fence post. I recall having once watched a pair of chickadees hollowing the upper end of a truncated sassafras tree that was half decayed. They would fly into the cavity, pick off a chip, dash out and away a rod or two, drop the fragment, then dart back to the hollow for another piece. In this way the busy couple worked hour by hour without resting for an instant. Their reason no doubt for carrying the chips some distance away from their nest was that they did not want any telltale fragments to betray their secret to their enemies.

It would be impossible to tell how many chickadee nests I have found in all the years of my bird study. One of them was in an old stump near a path along which I was sauntering. My attention was attracted by the little husband's flying from the stump and calling nervously, thus unwittingly "giving away" his secret. Had he been quiet, my suspicions would not have been aroused; but many birds, like a few people here and there, find it very hard to keep a secret. And this, by the way, is one of the strangest things about Nature--that she has not taught her feathered children to go with apparent unconcern about their employment when a nest is near, but impels them to chirp and flit about in such a way as to excite the suspicion of an enemy.

Moralizing aside, however. On examining the stump, I found a deep cavity just inside of the decaying bark. Though it was quite dusk within, by slightly pressing the bark aside I could see the little mother sitting on the nest, unwilling to leave it in spite of my proximity. I almost touched her with my hand, and still she did not move. Unwilling to disturb so brave a heroine, I stepped back and walked quietly away a few rods to see what would happen, when she popped out of the orifice like an arrow and, joined by her mate, set up a loud chattering, which sounded as if they were saying that I was the nosiest and most impudent man in the whole countryside.

No doubt they were right, for I went back, in spite of their protest, and peeped into the nest, and found four gleaming white eggs studding the bottom like pearls. Alas! when I visited the place two weeks later, the little domicile had been raided, the half-decayed walls having been broken down. A tuft of gray hair hanging to a splinter proved the invader to have been a predatory animal of some kind, probably a cat. The birds were nowhere to be seen--unless a pair chirping in the woods on the other side of the valley were the same couple, trying to rear a family in a safer place.

What a persistent sitter the female blackcap is! One day I discovered a nest in a fence post by the wayside. Pressing the bark aside, I could plainly see the little owner snuggling close to the bottom of the cup. I thrust my finger through the aperture and gently stroked her head and back. Still she hugged the nest, pressing her head close to the grassy bottom, as if she thought she would be safe if her head were hidden. Thinking she must have little ones, or she would not cling so tenaciously to the nest, I pushed my finger under her and partly raised her from her seat. Even this rude treatment she bore for a few moments--but it was going too far even for her courageous little heart; she lifted her head, glanced wildly at me for an intense moment, then sprang from the cavity with a piercing cry.

Imagine my surprise to find the nest entirely empty, not even an egg having yet been deposited. The brave little lady had doubtless just entered the nest to lay her first egg, and was not going to be driven off without knowing the reason why. The tomtit is game every time.

The entrance to most of the chickadee's nests is lateral, but I found one nest whose doorway was in the top of a fence post, so that the owners had to go down into it vertically. The hole was quite deep, and the birds would drop down into it as you have seen swifts dropping into a chimney, but whether they went down head first or tail first I could not learn, their movements were so quick. Another feature of this nest was that it had no roof, for the doorway was open to the sky, so that a cloudburst would have filled up their little nursery and drowned its inmates.

THE NUTHATCH FAMILY*

*This chapter is reprinted from that excellent bird magazine called "American Ornithology," published by Charles K. Reed, Worcester, Mass., and edited by his son, Chester A. Reed. The author is under obligation to these gentlemen for their courtesy in permitting him to reprint the article.

BIRDS OF THE INVERTED POSITION

There are a number of climbers in the bird realm, but none are quite so expert as the nuthatch, which may be regarded as a past-master in the art of clambering. The woodpeckers amble up the boles and branches of trees, and when they wish to descend, as they do occasionally for a short distance, they hitch down backward. The brown creepers ascend their vertical or oblique walls in the same way, but seldom, if ever, do anything else than clamber upward, never descending head downward after the fashion of the nuthatches.

Red-breasted Nuthatch

A little bird that comes very near disputing the palm with the nuthatch as a sylvan coaster is the creeping warbler, which flits about over the tree boles in all kinds of attitudes, even with his dainty head pointed toward the earth. No fear in his little striped breast of the blood rushing to his brain. However, even this clever birdlet's dexterity is not equal to that of the nuthatch, for the latter is able to climb up and down a smoother wall than his little rival. More than that, the nuthatch glides downward with more ease and in a straight line, and does not fling himself from side to side as the warbler does. Indeed, the warbler's favorite method of going about is with his head directed toward the sky rather than the reverse, while it really seems that the nuthatch's predilection is to scuttle about in an inverted position. Does he wish to chisel a grub out of the bark of a tree? He usually stands above the target at which he aims, so that he can deliver his blows with more force, just as the human woodchopper prefers to take his position above and not below the stick or log upon which he expects to operate. There the bird clings to his shaggy wall, pounding away with might and main, until you fear he will shatter his beak or strew his brains on the bark. Sometimes, too, he thrusts his long, slender beak into a crevice and pries with it in a way that threatens to snap it off in the middle.

What has been said applies to the white-breasted nuthatch (Sitta carolinensis), but it is fair to assume that all the other members of this subfamily behave in the same way. The woodpeckers and creepers use their spiny tails as supports while stationary or in motion; not so the nuthatches, which are sufficiently nimble on their feet to stand or glide without converting their tails into braces. Odd as it may seem to the uninformed, the nuthatches belong to the order of passeres or perching birds, in spite of their creeping habits. The systematists have placed them in this niche of the avicular scheme, not only because they are able to perch like other passeres on twigs and small branches, but also because they have the foot of the true perching bird, with three toes in front and one, well developed, in the rear. In this respect they differ again from the woodpeckers, which have either two fore and two hind toes, or two in front and only one behind. This will appear all the more remarkable when it is remembered that the Picidae do not descend head downward at all, while the Sittinae are the head-downward goers par excellence. Yet they have only one rear toe to support them in their inverted position. You would naturally suppose that if any bird had need of two hind toes, it would be the nuthatch; but the result proves that, after all, Nature had her wits about her when she evolved this avian family.

The world over, there are twenty distinct species of nuthatches known to scientific observers, but only four of them are natives of America. Of course, there are a number of subspecies or varieties. All of them are incessant climbers and foragers, peering into crannies, pounding here and there to make the grubs stir in their hiding places, jabbing and prying with their beaks, and chiseling out all kinds of larvae, grubs, and borers that would, if permitted to live and multiply, soon devastate the timber and fruit trees and make this world a desert indeed. True, the other feathered clamberers and carpenters are fully as useful, but depend upon it, the nuthatches do their share in preserving our forests and orchards.

The white-breasted nuthatch is our most common species east of the great plains, breeding from the Gulf States to the northern border of the United States and to New Brunswick. One peculiarity about him is that he breeds throughout his range, and therefore may be found as both a summer and winter resident in all suitable localities within these boundaries. In the winter, no matter how old Boreas may bluster, he is one of the most cheerful denizens of the woods in our central latitudes, calling his nasal "yank, yank, yank," and sometimes indulging in a loud, half-merry outburst that goes echoing through the woodlands. No sound of the sylvan solitudes has a more woodsy flavor or is more suggestive of vernal cheer and good will. Sometimes he chatters to his human visitors in the most cordial tones as he glides up and down his arboreal promenade, or holds himself almost straight out.

A hole in a stump or tree makes Madame Nuthatch a cosy nursery, which she lines with feathers and leaves, making it soft and snug for her downy brood. Here they are safe from most of the prowlers that find the more exposed nests of many other birds. She deposits five to eight eggs of a white or creamy-white ground-color, speckled with rufous and lavender. During the season of incubation and brood rearing the nuthatches retire to the depth of the woods, and are quiet, secretive, and unsocial, seldom betraying their procreant secrets.

These birds have another habit that is worth mentioning. Having found a larger supply of food than they require for their immediate use, they carry morsels away and jam them into all sorts of holes and crannies in the bark of the trees. I have watched a pair for an hour diligently laying by a store of sunflower seeds, which they had found at the edge of the woods. They do not store a quantity of provision in one place like the squirrels, but deposit a tidbit here and there, wedging it tightly into a crevice by hammering it with their stout bills. Of course, the woodpeckers and tomtits secure many of these half-hidden goodies, but Master Nuthatch does not mind that, for he evens up the theft by appropriating their stores when he finds them.

The white-breasted nuthatch may be known by his flat body and broad shoulders, his bluish gray coat, black cap and mantle (all in one piece), white cravat, shirt bosom and vest, with a few rufous decorations on the belly and under tail-coverts. The following quotations from Wilson are given as much for their vivacious manner as for the story itself:

"The male is extremely attentive to the female while sitting, supplying her regularly with sustenance, stopping frequently at the mouth of the hole, calling and offering her what he has brought, in the most endearing manner. Sometimes he seems to stop merely to inquire how she is, and to lighten the tedious moments with his soothing chatter. He seldom rambles far from the spot, and when danger appears, regardless of his own safety, he flies instantly to alarm her. When both are feeding on the trunk of the same tree, or of adjoining trees, he is perpetually calling on her; and, from the momentary pause he makes, it is plain he feels pleased to hear her reply.

"He rests and roosts with his head downwards; and appears to possess a degree of curiosity not common in many birds; frequently descending, very silently, within a few feet of the root of the tree where you happen to stand, stopping, head downward, stretching out his neck in a horizontal direction, as if to reconnoiter your appearance, and after several minutes of silent observation, wheeling around, he again mounts, with fresh activity, piping his unisons as before... Sometimes the rain, freezing as it falls, encloses every twig, and even the trunk of the tree, in a hard, transparent coat or shell of ice. On these occasions I have observed his anxiety and dissatisfaction at being with difficulty able to make his way along the smooth surface; at these times he generally abandons the trees, gleans about the stables, around the house, mixing among the fowls, entering the barn, and examining the beams and rafters, and every place where he may pick up a subsistence."

Our charming white-breast has a little cousin called the red-breasted nuthatch (Sitta canadensis), whose under parts are rufous or reddish buff instead of white. His crown and nape are black, then a white band runs back from the base of the upper mandible to the hind neck, and below this a black stripe reaches back in a parallel direction and encloses the eye. His upper parts, save those mentioned, are bluish gray. He is considerably smaller than the white-breast, and his range is more northerly in summer; but, unlike his cousin, he does not breed throughout his range; only in the localities which he selects for his summer home. Hence he is a migrant, dwelling in winter in the southern states, and in summer in the latitude of Manitoba and Maine and northward, and also on the summits of the mountains as far south as Virginia. It will be seen that the breeding precincts of the two species overlap, while in winter canadensis comes down from the north and takes up his abode in the southern part of the demesne of carolinensis.

While the white-breast is partial to oak, beech, maple, and other deciduous forests, his little relative prefers a woodland of pine, being very fond of scampering about on the cones, clinging to them with his strong claws, and extracting the seeds with his stout little bill. His call, though much like the "yank" of the white-breast, is pitched to a higher key, and has even a more pronounced nasal intonation, sounding as if he had taken a severe cold. Besides, he gives expression to some cheery notes that seem to be reserved for his own family or exclusive social circles. I found these pretty nuthatches in the pine woods on Mackinac Island in midsummer, and have good reason to believe that they breed there.

Cavities in trees or stumps furnish the redbreasts with nesting places suited to their taste; but they have a cunning way of plastering the entrance above and below with pine pitch, so as to make it just large enough to admit their tiny bodies and yet too small to let in their enemies. In this respect they steal the laurels from their white-breasted kinsmen, who seem to have no means by which to lessen the dimensions of their natural doorways.

A still smaller member of this group is the brown-headed nuthatch (Sitta pusilla), a resident of the South Atlantic and Gulf states, at rare intervals wandering "accidentally" as far north as Missouri and New York. A daintily dressed little fellow is this bird, the top and back of his head a dark grayish brown with a whitish patch on the nape, the remainder of his upper parts being bluish gray and his under parts grayish white. His favorite dwelling places are in the pine woods of the south, where he is on the most cordial terms socially with the pine warbler and the red-cockaded woodpecker. A most active little body, he scampers from the roots of the trees to the terminal twigs at the top, inspecting every cone, cranny and knot hole, chirping his fine, high-keyed notes, sometimes in a querulous tone, and again in the most cheerful and good-natured temper imaginable, now gliding up a tree trunk, now scudding down head foremost, anon circling in a spiral course.

One autumn I found a number of these nuthatches associated with a flock of myrtle warblers on the most sociable terms in a pine woodland not far from Pensacola, Florida. Now they were up in the trees, now down on the ground. All the while they were chirping in their most genial tones. In a spring jaunt to southern Mississippi, I was fortunate enough to find a nest in a half-decayed snag. It contained four of the prettiest half-fledged bird babies that have ever greeted my sight.

Oddly enough, our tiny clamberers utter a loud, shrill alarm-call that bears close resemblance to the querulous protest of the sparrow hawk as you approach her nest or young. Doctor Chapman says of the brown heads: "They are talkative sprites, and, like a group of school children, each one chatters away without paying the slightest attention to what his companions are saying."

The fourth member of the Sittinae subfamily in America is the pigmy nuthatch, known scientifically as Sitta pygmaea, a genuine westerner, not known east of the plains. However, in the Rocky Mountain district he is an abundant species, his range east and west being from the plains to the Pacific coast, and north and south from the Canadian boundary to the mountains of Mexico. Swinging and gliding about among the pines, performing the same antics as his eastern kinsmen, he utters a cheery whistle, that may be translated, "Whit, whit, whit." His movements are often so rapid that he is difficult to follow with the eye as he flits from one tree to another or dashes amid the branches. He scarcely remains quiet long enough for you to note his markings and settle his identity, but once you are sure of him, you will never mistake him for another bird.

In Colorado there is little of a migratory movement even up and down the mountains among these interesting birdlets. In the winter a few descend from the heights and dwell on the plains, where the weather is not so rigorous. On the approach of spring they again hie up into the mountains, spending the summer there and rearing their pretty bairns. However, the majority of them remain in the mountains all winter, braving the bitterest and fiercest storms, often at an altitude of 8,000 feet. Their breeding range is from 6,000 to 10,000 feet, the latter elevation being only a little below the timber line.

In spite of his unique and interesting habits, the poets have scarcely begun to chant the praises of the American nuthatch. One of the best tributes I have been able to find is from the pen of Edith Thomas, who apostrophizes our bird in this way:

"Shrewd little haunter of woods all gray, Whom I meet on my walk of a winter day, You're busy inspecting each cranny and hole In the ragged bark of yon hickory bole; You intent on your task, and I on the law Of your wonderful head and gymnastic claw!

"The woodpecker well may despair of this feat-- Only the fly with you can compete! So much is clear; but I fain would know How you can so reckless and fearless go, Head upward, head downward, all one to you, Zenith and nadir the same to your view."

We have now described the American nuthatch quartette, and will turn to other fields no less inviting, albeit more remote. The nuthatch of central Europe, scientifically known as Sitta caesia, is closely related to our American forms, resembling them in many of his habits. In studying the literature of the transatlantic species, we at once stumble upon the reason for calling this avian family by the somewhat peculiar and apparently inapt name of nuthatch. The older English form of the word was "nuthack," which unfortunately has been changed to "nuthatch," a word that gives an erroneous impression, for no bird ever hatches a nut. But with the last syllable "hack" the difficulty is all cleared up, as his habit of hacking or chipping nuts, which he places in chinks of the bark or wall, is well known.

The nuthatch of England belongs to the species just named. He does not wear a black hood or mantle, but merely a black ribbon on the side of his head, enclosing the eye. His upper parts are bluish gray, save the outer tail feathers, which are black; his cheeks and throat are white, his breast and belly buff, and his flanks and lower tail-coverts chestnut red. A graphic English writer, Dr. W. H. Hudson, gives the following enthusiastic description of the little tobogganist of his native woodlands:

"When I see him sitting quite still for a few moments on a branch of a tree in his most characteristic nuthatch attitude, on or under the branch, perched horizontally or vertically, with head or tail uppermost, but always with the body placed beetle-wise against the bark, head raised, and the straight, sharp bill pointed like an arm lifted to denote attention,--at such times he looks less like a living than a sculptured bird, a bird cut out of beautifully variegated marble--blue-gray, buff, and chestnut, and placed against the tree to deceive the eye. The figure is so smooth and compact, the tints so soft and stone-like; and when he is still, he is so wonderfully still, and his attitude so statuesque! But he is never long still and when he resumes his lively, eccentric, up-and-down and sidewise motions, he is interesting in another way. He is like a small woodpecker who has broken loose from the woodpecker's somewhat narrow laws of progression, preferring to be a law unto himself.

"Without a touch of brilliant color, the nuthatch is a beautiful bird on account of the pleasing softness and harmonious disposition of his tints; and, in like manner, without being a songster in the strict sense of the word, his voice is so clear and far-reaching and of so pleasing a quality, that it often gives more life and spirit to the woods and orchards and avenues he frequents than that of many true melodists. This is more especially the case in the month of March, before the migratory songsters have arrived, when he is most loquacious. A high pitched, clear, ringing note, repeated without variation several times, is his most often-heard call or song. He will sometimes sit motionless on his perch, repeating this call at short intervals, for half an hour at a time. Another bird at a distance will be doing the same, and the two appear to be answering one another. He also has another call, not so loud and piercing, but more melodious: a double note, repeated two or three times, with something liquid and gurgling in the sound, suggesting the musical sound of lapsing water. These various notes and calls are heard incessantly until the young are hatched, when the birds at once become silent."

The nesting habits of caesia are quite similar to those of our American forms, with the following interesting exception: The doorway of the cavity constituting the bird's domicile is plastered up with clay, made viscid by the nuthatch's glutinous saliva, leaving in the center a circular hole just large enough to afford entrance and exit for the little owner. Says the author quoted above: "When the sitting bird is interfered with, she defends her treasures with great courage, hissing like a wryneck, and vigorously striking at her aggressor with her sharp bill." Like our common white-breast, the British bird may be attracted to human dwellings by furnishing him a regular supply of food suited to his taste, and may grow so trustful as to come when called, and even to catch morsels thrown to him in the air. In the forest he often hammers so loudly on a resonant branch that his tattoo is mistaken for that of a woodpecker. The interior of the nest "contains a bed of dry leaves, or the filmy flakes of the inner bark of a fir or cedar, on which the eggs are laid."

In northern Europe another form of the nuthatch guild is found, known scientifically as Sitta europea, whose under parts are white without any washing of buff on the breast.

The Levant furnishes a most charming addition to the feathered brotherhood now under consideration. The scientific gentlemen have christened it Sitta syriaca, and its common name is the rock nuthatch, an appellation that is most appropriate, for its chosen haunts are rocky cliffs, over the faces of which it scuttles in the most approved nuthatch fashion, head up or down, as the whim seizes it, clinging with its sharp claws to the chinks, ledges, protuberances, and rough surfaces of the rocky walls. A little larger than its European cousin, its markings are quite similar. In Syria it is common as far north as the southern shores of the Black Sea. Although somewhat shy, it is described as having "sprightly manners and a clear, ringing trill." Odd indeed are some of nature's evolutions, I had almost said caprices, for the rock nuthatch is just as much at home and apparently just as happy on its bleak precipices as is our merry whitebreast in his umbrageous home in the oak or maple forest.

But what kind of nests do the rock nuthatches construct on their limestone walls? That is one of the most interesting features of the life of these birds. One writer[1] who has observed them in their native haunts describes the rock nuthatch as "an expert clay mixer and molder." The bird does not chisel out a nursery in the rock--no, indeed; his method of constructing his nest is as follows: Having found a little hollow or indentation on the rocky wall, he will erect a cap or dome of mortar over it, plastering the structure so firmly against the surface that no rain or storm or predaceous creeping thing can demolish it until long after it has been abandoned by the little architect. The circular base of the nest is ten or twelve inches in diameter. The dome is not entirely closed up, but a small orifice is left in the center, upon the edges of which a narrow neck or funnel, also made of mortar, is raised, the hole just large enough to admit the body of the bird. The funnel is about three inches long.

The building material employed is fine clay softened and glutinated with the bird's saliva and mixed with plant fibers, for the little mason does not believe in making bricks without straw. So well packed is the inch-thick wall that a stiff knife blade must be used to cut through it. While the natural color of the adobe cottage is ash-gray, and therefore harmonizes with the general hue of its surroundings, and also with the mezzotints of the builder, yet he sometimes decorates it with the gaily colored wings of moths caught in the chase and attached to the plaster while it is fresh. The rock nuthatch is as expert a mixer of mortar as the well-known cliff swallows of our own country, and his adobe dwellings bear a close resemblance to theirs.

It is interesting to note that the European nuthatch, while nesting regularly in tree cavities, sometimes also chooses the crannies of rocks, when he goes a little more extensively into the plastering business; but his skill is not so well developed as that of his oriental cousin, whose mud cottage is a model of its kind.

[1] The writer referred to is Mr. H. C. Tracy, to whose charming article in "The Wilson Bulletin," published at Oberlin, Ohio, I am indebted for all my material on the rock nuthatch.

A FEATHERED PARASITE*

*Reprinted from Appleton's "Popular Science Monthly," with additions.

Nothing could more clearly prove that a common law runs through the whole domain of Nature than the fact that in every division of her realm there seems to be a class of parasites. In the vegetable world, as is well known, there are various plants that depend wholly on other plants for the supply of their vital forces. And in the human sphere there are parasites in a very real and literal sense--men and women who rely upon the toil and thrift of others to sustain them in worthless idleness.

In view of the almost universal character of this law it would be strange if these peculiar forms of dependence did not appear in the avian community. We do find such developments in that department of creation. Across the waters there is one bird that has won an unenviable reputation as a parasite: the European cuckoo relies almost wholly on the efforts of its more thrifty neighbors to hatch and rear its young, and thereby perpetuate the species. Strangely enough, our American cuckoos are not given to such slovenly habits, but build their own nests and faithfully perform the duties of nidification, as all respectable feathered folk should. However, this parasitical habit breaks out, quite unexpectedly, it must be conceded, in another American family of birds entirely distinct from the cuckoo group.

In America the cowbird, often called the cow bunting, is the only member of the avian household that spirits its eggs into the nests of other birds. The theory of evolution can do little toward accounting for the anomaly, and even if it should venture upon some suggestions it would still be just as difficult to explain the cause of the evolution in this special group, while all other avian groups follow the law of thrift and self-reliance.

The cowbird belongs to the family of birds scientifically known as Icteridae, which includes such familiar species as the bobolinks, orioles, meadowlarks, and the various kinds of blackbirds, none of which, I am glad to say, are parasites. The name Molothrus has been given to the genus that includes the cowbirds. They are confined to the American continent, having no analogues in the lands across the seas. The same may be said, indeed, of the whole Icteridae family. It may be a matter of surprise to many persons that there are twelve species and subspecies of cowbirds in North and South America, for most of us are familiar only with the common cowbird (Molothrus ater) of our temperate regions. Of these twelve species only three are to be found within the limits of the United States, one is a resident of western Mexico and certain parts of Central America, while the rest find habitat exclusively in South America. A fresh field of investigation is open to some enterprising and ambitious naturalist who wishes to study several of these species, as comparatively little is known of their habits, and indeed much still remains to be learned of the whole genus, familiar as one or two of the species are. Their sly, surreptitious manners render them exceedingly difficult to study at close range and with anything like satisfactory detail.

Are all of them parasites? Probably they are--at least to a greater or less degree--

except one, the bay-winged cowbird of South America, which I shall reserve for notice later on in this chapter. We might assert that our common cowbirds are the parasites par excellence of the family, for, so far as I can learn from reading and observation, they never build their own nests or rear their own young, but shift all the duties of maternity, save the laying of the eggs, upon the shoulders of other innocent birds.

These avian "spongers" have a wide geographical range, inhabiting the greater part of the United States and southern Canada, except the extensive forest regions and some portions of the southern states. They are most abundant in the states bordering on the upper Mississippi River and its numerous tributaries. On the Pacific coast west of the Cascade and Sierra Nevada mountains, they occur only as stragglers. The most northern point at which they have been known to breed is the neighborhood of Little Slave Lake in southern Athabaska. In the autumn the majority of these birds migrate to southern Mexico, although a considerable number remain in our southern states, and a few occasionally tarry for the winter even as far north as New England and southern Michigan.

The male cowbird looks like a well-dressed gentleman--and may have even a slightly clerical air--in his closely fitting suit of glossy black, with its greenish and purplish iridescence, and his hood of rich metallic brown covering his head, neck, and chest. He makes a poor shift as a musician, but his failure is not due to lack of effort, for during courtship days he does his level best to sing a variety of tunes, expanding and distorting his throat, fluffing up his feathers, spreading out his wings and tail, his purpose evidently being to make himself as fascinating as possible in the eyes of his lady love. One of his calls sounds like "spreele," piped in so piercing a key that it seems almost to perforate your brain.

One observer maintains that the cowbirds are not only parasitical in their habits, but are also absolutely devoid of conjugal affection, practicing polyandry, and seldom even mating. This is a serious charge, but it is doubtless true, for even during the season of courtship and breeding these birds live in flocks of six to twelve, the males almost always outnumbering the females. However, if their family relations are somewhat irregular, no one can accuse them of engaging in brawls, as so many other birds do, for both males and females seem to be on the most amicable terms with one another, and are, to all appearances, entirely free from jealousy. Who has ever seen two cowbirds fighting a duel like the orioles, meadowlarks, and robins?

In obtruding her eggs into the nests of other birds, Madame Cowbird is sly and stealthy. She does not drive the rightful owners from their nests, but simply watches her opportunity to drop her eggs into them when they are unguarded. No doubt she has been on the alert while her industrious neighbors have been constructing their domiciles, and knows where almost every nest in the vicinity is hidden. Says Major Charles Bendire: "In rare instances only will a fresh cowbird's egg be found among incubated ones of the rightful owners. I have observed this only on a single occasion." From one to seven eggs of the parasite are found in the nests of the dupes. In most cases the number is two, but in the case of ground builders the cowbird seems to have little fear of overdoing her imposition. Major Bendire says that he once found the nest of an oven-bird containing seven cowbird's eggs and only one of the little owner's.

If parasitism were the only crime of the cowbird one would not feel so much disposed to put her into the Newgate Calendar; but she not only inflicts her own eggs upon her innocent victims, but often actually tosses their eggs out of the nests in order to make room for her own. Nor is that all; she will sometimes puncture the eggs of the owners to prevent their hatching, and thus increase the chances of her own offspring. Whether this is done with her beak or her claws is still an open question, Major Bendire inclining to the belief that it is done with the claws.

Her finesse is still further to be seen in the fact that she usually selects some bird for a victim that is smaller than herself, so that when her young hopefuls begin to grow they will be able to crowd or starve out the true heirs of the family. In this way it is thought that many a brood comes to an untimely end, the foster parents having no means of replacing their own little ones when they have been ejected from the nest. However, I doubt whether the cowbird's impositions are usually so destructive as some observers are inclined to believe. I once found a bush sparrow's nest containing one cowbird and four little sparrows, all of which were in a thriving condition. The sparrows were so well fed and active that as soon as I touched the nest they sprang, with loud chirping, over the rim of their cottage and scuttled away through the grass. They were certainly strong and healthy, in spite of the presence of their big foster brother. Before they flitted away I had time to notice how the little family were disposed. The cowbird was squatted in the center of the nest, while his little foster brothers and sisters were ranged around him, partly covering him and no doubt keeping him snug and warm. They were further advanced than he, for while they scrambled from the nest, he could do nothing but snuggle close on the bottom of the cup.

A wood thrush's nest that I found contained two young thrushes and two buntings. All of them were about half fledged. Being of nearly the same size, the queerly assorted bantlings lived in apparent peace in their narrow quarters. I watched them at frequent intervals, but saw no attempts on the part of the foundlings to crowd out their fellow-nestlings. The cowbirds were the first to leave the sylvan roof tree. Thus it appears that the intrusion of the cowbird's eggs does not always mean disaster to the real offspring of the brooding family, but of course it often prevents the laying of the full complement of eggs by the builders themselves.

Even after the youngsters have left the nest the mother cowbird does not assume the care of them, but still leaves them in charge of the foster parents. It is laughable, almost pathetic, to see a tiny oven-bird or redstart feeding a strapping young cowbird which is several times as large as herself. She looks like a pigmy feeding a giant. In order to thrust a tidbit into his mouth she must often stand on her tiptoes. Why the diminutive caterer does not see through the fraud I can not say. She really seems to be attached to the hulking youngster. By and by, however, when he grows large enough to shift for himself, he deserts his little parents and nurses and seeks companionship among his own blood kindred, who doubtless bring him up in the way all cowbirds should go.

It is surprising how many species are imposed on successfully by the cowbird. The number, so far as has been observed, is ninety, with probably more to be added. Among the birds most frequently victimized are the phoebes, the song sparrows, the indigo birds, the bush sparrows, and the yellow-breasted chats. Even the nests of the red-headed woodpecker and the rock wrens are not exempt. Some species, notably the summer warblers, detect the imposture and set about defeating the purposes of the interloper by building another story to their little cottage, leaving the obtruded eggs in the cellar, where they do not receive enough warmth to develop the embryo.

While it is surprising that acute birds should allow themselves to be imposed on in this way, perhaps, after all, they look upon the cowbird as a kind of blessing in disguise; at least, he may not be an unmixed evil. They may act on the principle of reciprocity--that "one good turn deserves another." What I mean is this: In my rambles I have often found the cowbirds the first to give warning of the approach of a supposed danger. Having no domestic duties of their own, they can well secrete themselves in a tall tree overlooking the entire premises, and thus play the useful role of sentinel. This, I am disposed to believe, is one of the compensating uses of this parasite, and may furnish the reason for his being tolerated in birdland. And he is tolerated. Has any one ever seen other birds driving the cowbird away from their breeding precincts, or charging him with desperate courage, as they do the blue jays, the hawks, the owls, and other predatory species? He evidently subserves some useful purpose in the avian community, or he would not be treated with so much consideration.

A young cowbird that I purloined from the nest and tried to rear by hand did not prove a pleasant pet. He was placed in a large cage with several other kinds of young birds. At first he was quite docile, taking his food from my hand and even allowing some of his feathered companions to feed him; but in a few weeks he grew so wild and manifested such a fierce desire for the outdoor world that I was glad to carry him out to the woods and give him his freedom. A young red-winged blackbird and a pair of meadowlarks developed a different disposition.

The dwarf cow-bird (Molothrus ater obscurus) is similar to his relative just described, except that he is smaller and his geographical range is more restricted. He is a resident of Mexico, southern Texas, southwestern Arizona, and southern California. His habits resemble those of the common cowbird. Another bunting having almost the same range, although a little more southerly, is the red-eyed cowbird, which is larger and darker than our common cowbird and has the same parasitical habits.

In South America three species have been studied by Mr. W. H. Hudson, who, in collaboration with Mr. P. L. Sclater, has published a most valuable work on Argentine ornithology. One of these is called the Argentine cowbird (Molothrus bonariensis). It is a blue-blooded parasite, and has been seen striking its beak into the eggs of other birds and flying away with them. The males, it is said, show little discrimination in pecking the eggs, for they are just as likely to puncture the cowbird eggs as those of other birds. Every egg in a nest is frequently perforated in this way. These buntings lay a large number of eggs, often dropping them on the ground, laying them in abandoned nests, or depositing them in nests in which incubation has already begun, in which case all of them are lost. However, in spite of this wastefulness the birds thrive, thousands of them being seen in flocks during the season of migration.

And, by the way, a description of their habits by Mr. Hudson has thrown interesting light on the subject of migration in the southern hemisphere. South of the equator the recurrence of the seasons is the exact reverse of their recurrence north of the equator, and therefore the breeding season of the birds is in the autumn instead of the spring; the flight from winter cold occurs in the spring instead of in the autumn, and is toward the north instead of toward the south. Thus, in February and March the Argentine cowbirds are seen flying in vast battalions in the direction of the equatorial regions-- that is, northward--in whose salubrious clime they spend the winter. As our northern autumn draws near and the southern spring approaches these winged migrants take the air line for their breeding haunts in the Argentine Republic and Patagonia. At the same time the migrants of the northern hemisphere are pressing southward before the blustering north wind. It all seems wonderful and solemn, this world-wide processional of the seasons and the birds.

Naturally one would expect to find some other eccentricities in this aberrant family besides that of parasitism, and in this expectation one is not disappointed. There are two other species of cowbirds in the Argentine country--the screaming cowbird (Molothrus rufoaxillaris) and the bay-winged cowbird (Molothrus badius). The latter is only partly a trencher on the rights of other birds--only half a parasite. Indeed, it sometimes builds its own nest, which is quite a respectable affair; but, as if to prove that it still has some remnants of cowbird depravity in its nature, it frequently drives other birds from their rightful possessions, appropriates the quarters thus acquired, lays its eggs into them, and proceeds to the performance of its domestic duties like its respectable neighbors. Its virtue is that it never imposes the work of incubation and brood rearing on any of its feathered associates, even though it does sometimes eject them from their premises.

But what is to be said of the screaming cowbird? Instead of inflicting its eggs on its more distant avian relatives, it watches its chance and slyly drops them into the domicile of its bay-winged cousins, and actually makes them hatch and rear its offspring! This seems to be carrying imposture to the extreme of refinement, or possibly developing it into a fine art, and reminds one of those human good-for-naughts who "sponge" off their relatives rather than go among strangers.

Before closing this chapter I must call attention to one of the most surprising discoveries ever made by an American observer of bird ways. It was reported some time after my article on the cowbird was first published in Appleton's "Popular Science Monthly." The observer was Joseph F. Honecker, whose statement was printed in "American Ornithology" for June, 1902, and runs as follows:

"As ornithologists and all bird students think and believe that the cowbird will build no nest, but always lays in the nests of other birds, I am glad to give the results of my experiments. In order to get the desired results, in the spring of 1899 I secured a pair of cowbirds and placed them in a large cage, cared well for them, and supplied them with plenty of nesting material. To my surprise, the female built a nest, laid four eggs, hatched them, and reared the young, and on July twenty-eighth, young and old were given their freedom. This will show that the cowbird will build a nest and care for its young in captivity, while in its wild life it has never been known to do so."

A BLUE CANNIBAL*

*Reprinted by permission from "The Evening Post," New York.

In his coat of light blue, trimmed with white and black, bearing his crest jauntily atop of his head, the blue jay presents an attractive picture. And, indeed, although I myself feel that the Baltimore oriole, the scarlet tanager, the ruby-throated hummingbird, and many of the wood warblers carry off the palm for brilliancy of plumage, there are persons who declare that the jay is the most handsomely colored bird in our temperate regions.

While the jay dons an engaging attire, not much can be said in the way of eulogy for his vocal talents or acquirements. Many of his calls are harsh, penetrating, and even raucous. Frequently, too, he indulges in a great to-do over nothing, fairly splitting your ears with his noisy cries. I have said it is a to-do over nothing, though Mr. Jay may think he has the best reason in the world for making a fuss. Often espying some coveted prize on the ground in my back yard, instead of quietly dropping down and taking it, he and his companions would dash about in the trees, swing their bodies sidewise and up and down in an excited way, and scream at the top of their voices, sometimes drawing me out of the house to see what had gone wrong in Jaydom. They seemed to be determined to attract the attention of every person on the premises to the fact that they wanted that morsel on the ground, but were afraid to venture down after it. Perhaps they meant by their objurgations to test their human neighbors, to ascertain whether any of them were prowling about with a gun or a sling, ready to do them harm. If there should be any such prowlers, probably the jays meant to induce them to come out of their ambush, to show themselves in the open, and give their jayships a chance to escape. Bird psychology, as you will have occasion to note more than once, is a good deal of an enigma. How often we would give a handsome bonus to a bird if he would let us know precisely what he was thinking about!

Although no musician, the jay has quite an extensive vocal repertory. Besides his loud, challenging call, he frequently utters a series of calls that have a pensive quality and that fill the mind with an indefinable foreboding, especially on chill autumn days when all the woods are bare and gray and the wind is moaning through the boughs. Sometimes when a jay is hidden in a copse, he utters a low, scolding sputter, that seems to express the very quintessence of disgust. It is simply his way of telling you what he thinks of a man who goes prowling about without leave in the precincts of the birds.

Blue Jay

Have you ever heard the jay's brief musical roulade? It is only a wisp of melody, rarely rich and suggestive, heard a moment, then gone. You know something sweet has passed by, but something so brief and elusive that you scarcely know what it was. Long after it has dropped on your ear, it continues to haunt your memory, and you try again and again to reproduce it, but in vain. It has a kind of gurgling quality, as if the bird were pressing his notes through an aqueous lyre, if such a conception is possible. Besides, I have, on more than one occasion, heard a jay warble a soft, reserved little lay that was continued for many minutes. It sounded very like the song of the brown thrasher, much modulated and partly uttered under its breath--a sort of flowing, rythmical melody.

A question that disturbs all bird lovers more or less is this: Does the fine white vest of the jay cover a bad heart? Is he really a thief, a nest robber, or even worse, a cannibal, in plumes? May the guardian spirit of all feathered folk forbid that I should blacken the reputation of any bird, yet honesty compels me to give an affirmative answer to the foregoing question. I hasten, however, to say that I do not believe he is as black as he has been painted by some observers, who seem to delight in making out a verdict of capital guilt against him. Although a predatory bird, he is not engaged all the time in bloodthirsty pursuits, but only while his young are in the nest clamoring for food. What are some of the proofs of his vandalism? I will mention a few of them.

First, almost all the small birds make uncompromising war upon him, especially in the breeding season, and many of them show signs of dire distress when he goes near their nests. They often utter pitiful cries, droop their wings, and the bravest of them dash at him savagely, giving him many a cuff on the head and back. The wood pewee and the kingbird succeed, I think, in driving him away; but the vireos and warblers, being so much smaller, suffer greatly from his depredations. If there were no real cause for it, these birds would not be filled with panic and rage on account of the jay's presence. There is strong presumptive evidence that they know him for an outlaw only too well.

The following incident will furnish positive proof of the jay's cannibalistic proclivities: One spring my little boy brought home from the country a young house wren, thinking it would make a delightful pet. It was quite well fledged, but its short tail and white mouth border proclaimed the tenderness of its youth. Fearing that the little thing could not be reared by hand, as it refused all our proffered tidbits, and chirped continually for its parents, I persuaded the lad to give it its freedom. A mother wren living on our premises seemed inclined to adopt the little waif, and we decided to put it under her care. No sooner was the youngling let out of the cage than it flew to the side of the house and began to scramble up the brick wall. It had a hard tug, but at length succeeded in reaching a resting place on a window-shutter of the second story.

Presently the mother wren heard its calls and paid it a visit; but instead of feeding it, she seemed very anxious to drive it away, knowing, no doubt, that there were predaceous enemies in the neighborhood. In her attempts to drive it into hiding, she pecked it on the head and in the mouth. Then she dropped down into a thicket and secured a green worm, with which she flew up to the chirping waif's perch; but I could not make out that she fed the birdling, though she thrust the worm toward its open mouth. Soon after she had gone off the second time, the little bird clambered around the corner of the wall to the lower side of the house, where it rested a while on a narrow shelf.

All this time my boy and I were watching it intently. Suddenly a blue jay came flying over from one of the trees of an adjacent yard, moving in a rapid, stealthy way. First it plunged into an apple tree at the corner of the house; then, before I could collect my wits enough to know what was happening, it darted over to the brick wall, seized the little wren with its bill, and bore it off. The mother wren followed, uttering a pitiful chatter, while the little victim called loudly for help. The blue kidnapper darted to a tree in my neighbor's yard, where he put his booty under his claw on a limb, holding it by one slender leg, while its body dangled below. Hoping still to rescue the little captive, I sprang over into the adjacent yard with a loud shout and much waving of my hands; but my vigorous efforts only caused the jay to pick up the wren in its bill and continue its flight, and neither wren nor jay was seen by me again. This incident furnishes unimpeachable testimony against the character of the blue-coated Robin Hood. There was no faltering or hesitancy in his conduct, but he seized and carried off his little victim as if he were to the manner born, and had become hardened by practice in depredations of the sort.

A farmer once related the following incident to me: A pair of chipping sparrows had built a nest in a bush in his front yard. One day after the little ones had arrived, he heard a distressed chirping coming from the parent birds, and on going to the front yard, he caught a blue jay in the act of picking a callow bantling from the chippie's nest. Holding it in his bill, the jay flew across the field with his prize, and presently returned and bore off a second nestling. By this time the farmer's ire was aroused; he bolted into the house and secured his shotgun, and when the marauding jay came back on the third trip on robbery intent, the man brought him to the ground with a shot that ended his career.

Yet the jay is not wholly bad--indeed, not even half bad. Before me lies a valuable pamphlet entitled "The Blue Jay and His Food," written by F. E. L. Beal, Assistant Biologist of the Department of Agriculture at Washington, whose researches have converted him into something of an apologist for our blue gentleman in feathers. He dissected the stomachs of 292 jays, collected during every month of the year in twenty-two states, the District of Columbia, and Canada. After stating that mineral substances in the stomachs examined averaged over 14 per cent of the total contents, Mr. Beal says:

"The real food is composed of 24.3 per cent of animal matter and 75.7 per cent of vegetable matter, or a trifle more than three times as much vegetable as animal. The animal food is chiefly made up of insects, with a few spiders, myriapods, snails, and small vertebrates, such as fish, salamanders, tree frogs, mice, and birds. Everything was carefully examined which might by any possibility indicate that birds or eggs had been eaten, but remains of birds were found in only two, and the shells of small birds' eggs in only three of the 292 stomachs. One of these, taken on February tenth, contained the bones, claws, and a little skin of a bird's foot. Another, taken on June twenty-fourth, contained the remains of a young bird. The three stomachs with bird's eggs were collected in June, August, and October, respectively. The shell eaten in October belonged to the egg of some larger bird like the ruffed grouse and, considering the time of year, was undoubtedly merely an empty shell from an old nest. Shells of eggs which were identified as those of domesticated fowls, or some bird of equal size, were found in eleven stomachs, collected at irregular times during the year. This evidence would seem to show that more eggs of domesticated fowls than of wild birds are destroyed, but it is much more probable that these shells were obtained from refuse heaps about farm-houses."

Mr. Beal's dissections are very significant, proving that the jay is not only not so destructive of eggs and bantlings as was supposed, but also that he destroys many noxious insects, and is, therefore, a bird of real economic value. The great bulk of his insect diet consists of beetles, grasshoppers, and caterpillars, with a few bugs, wasps, and flies, and an occasional spider and myriapod. The average of insect food for the whole year was 23 per cent, varying from less than 1 per cent in January to over 66 per cent in August, and it is gratifying to know that predaceous beetles and tent caterpillars form a large part of the jay's bill of fare.

His demands upon domesticated fruits and grains are comparatively light. He cares more for acorns and mast than for corn. The last he does not greatly relish, but eats it chiefly when the snow covers his favorite food. It is a little surprising that he occasionally varies his diet with fish, salamanders, tree frogs, mice, and shrews. Mr. Beal's conclusion is put in the following sentence, which closes his valuable monograph: "In fact, the examination of nearly three hundred stomachs shows that the blue jay does far more good than harm."

An important question, therefore, from more than one point of view is: Should we ever kill the blue jay? Perhaps as sensible an answer to that question as can be given is this: We should by no means engage in a war of extermination upon the jays, but it might be wise, when they become too abundant, to thin out their numbers somewhat by shooting some of them or driving them away. It can scarcely be denied that if they are permitted to thrive without hindrance, and grow to large numbers, they will become sorely destructive of the eggs and nestlings of more desirable birds. I assure you, however, that I make this statement with reluctance and reserve, for the handsome blue-coat is one of our most cunning and interesting birds, and would be greatly missed if he were exterminated.

The blue jay is also a plucky bird, as I discovered one day not so very long ago. A pair of jays had a nest in a little park in front of my house, and one day one of the youngsters, which were still unable to fly, dropped to the ground. Fearing the cats or evilly disposed boys might catch the little fellow, I thought to do him and his parents a good turn by catching him and putting him up in one of the trees beyond the reach of his enemies. After quite a chase I succeeded in catching him. But the parent birds, flitting and calling in the trees, did not understand my well-meant intentions, and so one of them swung down and struck me on the top of the head with so much force that, either with his bill or his claws; he punctured the skin and made the blood come, leaving a scar on my crown for quite a while. The pesky thing! I think he might have known that I was his friend--but he didn't, his instinct not being a sure guide that time. But who can blame him? Not an hour afterwards the youngling again fell to the ground, when some children found it and killed it without the least excuse for their action. In such a case how could the parent birds distinguish between friend and foe? They found their little one lying dead on the ground, and mourned for it with heart-broken cries.

Some things cause a great to-do in the jay world. One day, while I was living in Kansas, the skeleton of a jay, with the feathers still attached, was found in the rubbish of an ash-pile in my rear yard, and exposed to view. An hour later a half dozen or more jays were flinging about in the peach tree above the feathers of their dead comrade, screaming at the top of their voices, "juking" their bodies, as is their wont when excited, and glaring at the disheveled plumes on the ground. If it was a funeral service, it certainly was a demonstrative one, and I do not believe that their grief and terror were affected.

A HANDSOME SCISSORSTAIL*

*Reprinted by permission from "American Ornithology," with important additions.

In order to study the scissorstailed flycatcher (Milvulus forficatus), of which some friends had told me again and again in a glow of enthusiasm, I made a trip to southern Kansas and northern Oklahoma. Several days passed before an individual of this species put in appearance, as the scissorstails, which are migrants, had not yet returned from their winter quarters in a more southern clime, and so I had to wait for their arrival.

One day a friend and I were driving along a country road over the prairie, when a quaint bird form went swinging from the wire fence by the roadside toward a clump of willows in a shallow dip of the prairie. Dashing after him, I heard a clear, musical call that proclaimed a bird with which I had not yet become acquainted.

In a few moments he flew from the tree. My binocular was fixed upon him as he went flitting across the field and presently alighted on the ground. My surmise was correct; it was the scissorstail flycatcher, one of the most unique and handsome birds belonging to our American avifauna, one that merits more than a passing notice. To see him perched on a fence, or swinging gracefully through the air, and hear his bell-like calls and whistles makes you feel as if you were suddenly transported to a foreign land, like Australia or Borneo, where so many feathered curios are to be found.

In a fever of excitement I followed the bird, which presently flew back to the fence by the roadside. He flitted from point to point as my friend and I slowly pursued him, giving us an exhibition of his scissoring process. Sometimes he would alight on a post, then on the barbed wire, usually sitting flat on his breast. When open, the tail is bicolored, the outer border all around being white and the inner black. His general color is hoary ash, paler, almost white, below, giving out a slight iridescence in the sunshine; his wings are blackish, with white trimmings; his flanks are stained with salmon-red, and when his wings are spread, there appears a large blotch of scarlet at the inner angle of the intersection with the body. One individual that I afterwards saw wore a scarlet epaulet, which was almost concealed by the other plumes when the wing was closed, but was clearly seen when it was extended. An orange or scarlet gem adorns the crown, but is so well hidden by the other crest feathers that it is seldom noticed.

My friend and I were privileged to witness a rare and attractive scissorstail show, more gratifying than any circus performance. A loggerhead shrike suddenly appeared on the scene, and made an assault on the flycatcher. The two birds went gyrating, zigzagging, see-sawing through the air in a perfect jumble of white and black and ash. It must be remembered that the shrike himself makes a handsome picture on the wing, and when you come to mix up a scissorstail and a shrike in inextricable confusion, you have a feathery display worth seeing.

Nor was that the end of the exhibition, for in a moment a second scissorstail, the precise facsimile of the first, appeared from somewhere, and the two flycatchers combined against their enemy. Then for a few minutes there was such a chaos of shrike and scissorstail that we could scarcely tell which was which. By and by the shrike wheeled away, when, as if to bring the gladiatorial show to a climax, the scissorstails engaged in a set-to that was really wonderful, coming together in the air, whirling around and around, rising in a spiral course, opening and closing their beautiful forked tails in quick succession, the black and white trimmings flashing momentarily, then disappearing, until the contestants finally descended, parted in the most graceful manner, and alighted on separate fence posts, none the worse for their melee.

In the evening I returned to the enchanted spot, but the scissorstails had disappeared.

Not having had my fill of these charmers, I stopped, on my return home, for a day at Wellington, Kansas, where I was so fortunate as to find three birds of this species, who permitted me to watch them to my heart's content. They are not shy birds, but fly in a graceful, leisurely way from post to post along the fence as you walk or drive, sometimes sitting quietly to let you pass by. In this respect their habits are much like those of their cousin, the kingbird.

As his name indicates, our bird is the proud possessor of a genuine scissorstail, composed of two long, slender prongs that are spread far apart under certain conditions of flight. Let me describe the process minutely, for it is unique here in North America where fork-tailed birds are rare.

When the bird starts up from a perch, he spreads apart the prongs of his tail for a moment, as if to give himself a spring; then he closes them in a single slender stem, tapering outward to a point, keeping them closed during prolonged flight, and just as he sweeps down to another perch, he opens his ornamental scissors again, shutting them up as soon as he has settled upon his resting place. He does not open and close his tail at regular intervals during flight, as might be supposed, but keeps it closed until he descends to a perch, when it is opened for a moment in the act of alighting. However, if he has occasion to wheel or make a sudden turn in the air, either for an insect or in a playful prank, his scissors fly open, one might almost say spontaneously, no doubt serving the double purpose of rudder and balancing pole. When closed, the tail is very narrow, looking almost like a single plume. On the perch (except when he desires to shift his position, when he also makes use of his wings) his tail is closed. Therefore the picture of this bird in Dr. Coues's "Key to North American Birds" is not accurate, for it represents our bird in the sitting posture with the tines of his fork spread apart. If the wings were outstretched, representing the bird in the act of alighting or shifting his position, the picture would be true to scissorstail life.

The range of these birds is somewhat restricted, and for that reason, doubtless, so little is known about their habits. According to Ridgway, their proper home is in eastern Mexico and the southwestern prairie districts of the United States, though many of them come north as far as southern Kansas and southwestern Missouri to spend the summer and rear their families. In winter they go as far south as Costa Rico. Restricted as their habitat is, it is curious to note that they are "accidental" in a few unexpected places, such as Key West, Fla., Norfolk, Va., and also in several localities in New England, Manitoba, and Hudson Bay Territory. Prof. W. W. Cooke, of Colorado, says they are "rare, if not accidental," in that state. To show that our birds are unique, it is relevant to say that there are only two species of scissors-tailed flycatchers in North America, which have the genus Milvulus all to themselves. The other member of the genus is the forked-tailed flycatcher (Milvulus tyrannus), a resident of tropical America, migrating north normally as far as southern Mexico. He is a sort of southern twin of our scissorstail.

The nests of the scissorstails are set in the crotches of trees in the neighborhood of country homes on the prairie. Considering the size of the birds, their nests are quite small, not so large as those of the brown thrashers, though the cup is deeper and the architecture more compact and elaborate. A friend describes a nest which he found on a locust tree about sixteen feet from the ground. It was made mostly of dry grass and locust blossoms, with here and there a piece of twine braided into the structure. It had no special lining, but the grass was more evenly woven on the inside of the cup than elsewhere.

From three to five eggs are deposited. The ground color is white, either pure or creamy, sparingly mottled with rich madder-brown and lilac-gray, the spots being thicker and larger on the larger end. While the nest is undergoing examination, the owners circle and hover overhead, much after the fashion of the red-winged blackbirds, expressing their disapproval in loud and musical calls, and displaying their rich scarlet decorations.

My descriptions have related only to the male bird, whose beautiful forked tail is nine to ten inches long, and whose colors are clear and more or less intense. His spouse resembles him, but is slightly smaller, while her tail, though forked like her mate's, is from two and a half to three inches shorter. The salmon and scarlet ornaments on the sides, flanks, and axillars are paler than those of her lord, and the scarlet spot shows very indistinctly on her occiput. The young of both sexes don the dress of the mother bird during the first season, save that they fail to adorn themselves with a scarlet gem on the crown.

Like all the members of the flycatcher group, the scissorstails capture insects while on the wing, making many an attractive picture as they perform their graceful and interesting evolutions in the air.

It was a year or two later that I saw a scissorstail performing his ablutions in the northwestern part of Arkansas. How do you suppose he went about it? Not in the way birds usually do, by squatting down in the shallow water, twinkling their wings and tail, and sprinkling the liquid all over their plumage. No; this bird has a reputation to maintain for originality, and therefore he took his bath in this manner: First he perched on a telegraph wire by the roadside; then he swung gracefully down to a little pond, dashed lightly into the water, giving himself a slight wetting, after which he flew up to his original perch on the wire. A minute or less was then spent in preening his plumes; but they were not moist enough to suit his purpose, so he darted down to the pond again, making the spray rise as lie struck the water; then up to his perch he swung again, to arrange his feathers; and this was repeated a number of times, till his toilet was completed. It would not be safe to risk saying that the scissorstail always takes his bath in this way; but I know this one did. I once saw a kingbird doing the same thing, and so it may be a fashion in flycatcher circles.

I am minded, in order to make this monograph more complete, to borrow a couple of paragraphs from Mrs. Bailey's "Handbook of Birds of the Western United States." She has studied the bird in the Southwest, and gives the following graphic description of the bird and its habits:

"One of his favorite performances is to fly up and, with rattling wings, execute an a 雛 ial seesaw, a line of sharp-angled VVVVVVV's, helping himself at the short turns by rapidly opening and shutting his long white scissors. As he goes up and down he utters all the while a penetrating scream, Ka-quee-ka-quee-ka-quee-ka-quee-ka-quee, the emphasis being given each time at the top of the ascending line.

"Frequently when he is passing along with the even flight of a sober-minded crow, and you are quietly admiring the salmon lining of his wings, he shoots rattling into the air, and, as you stare after him, drops back as suddenly as he rose. He does this apparently because the spirit moves him, as a boy slings a stone at the sky, but fervor is added by the appearance of a rival or an enemy, for he is much like a Tyrannus in his masterful way of controlling the landscape. He will attack caracaras and white-necked ravens, lighting on their backs and giving them vicious blows while screaming in their ears."

AN ALPINE ROSY FINCH*

*Part of the material used in this chapter has already appeared in the author's work entitled "Birds of the Rockies," but it is here printed in different form, that of a monograph, with a number of additional facts. The writer feels that the readers of the present volume will relish at least a taste of bird study among the alpine heights of the Rocky Mountains. The article is reprinted from the "Denver Post," whose courtesy is hereby acknowledged.

The common name of the subject of this sketch is the brown-capped rosy finch; in the scientific works on ornithology he is called the brown-capped leucosticte. He is certainly a bird of peculiar habits and out-of-the-way preferences. Should he send you his card from his summer residence, it would read something like this: "At home in the mountains of Colorado, from 10,000 feet above sea-level to the summits of the highest peaks." There is only one other bird in Colorado that has so high a summer range, and that is the white-tailed ptarmigan, usually called, in hunter's parlance, the "mountain quail."

The rosy finch is slightly larger than the bluebird. His general color is light brown, suffused with a beautiful pink or rosy tint, the dark shaft lines and pale edges of the feathers of the back giving it a striped appearance. The forepart of the top of the head is blackish, and the cap is brown, from which he gets the qualifying adjective of his name. In the best nuptial plumage the rosy coloring is heightened to an intense crimson, especially on the wings, tail coverts, and the under parts. The female's attire is paler and duller of tint, the pink being sometimes almost obsolete. Oddly enough, in summer the bills of these birds are deep black, while in winter they become yellow, only the tip remaining black or blackish.

My introduction to the leucostictes occurred on the summit of Pikes Peak, at an elevation of 14,147 feet above the level of the sea. With exhausting toil I climbed the peak one night, and the next morning, when I stepped out of the signal station, where I had secured lodging, a flock of the brown-caps were flitting merrily about the garbage heap, helping themselves to an early breakfast. Their blithe chirping sounded very much like conversation all among themselves, and proclaimed two pleasant traits of character--cheerfulness and good temper. It was evident that they were happy and contented in their alpine home, in the upper story of the world, the rare, cool, exhilarating air, the majestic panoramas, and the unlimited freedom all contributing to the blithesomeness of their spirits. The keepers of the signal station told me that the birds came to the refuse pile every day for their meals.

Two years later, on the twenty-eighth of June, a friend and I clambered up Grays Peak, which is several hundred feet higher than Pikes Peak. It was a long and toilsome climb, winding about the snowbeds of the mountain side. Sometimes we scaled straight up the acclivity on "all fours," throwing ourselves down on the rocks at frequent intervals to rest our aching limbs and fill our lungs with the rarefied air; up and up and up, until at last, with a long pull and a strong pull, we stood on the sky-haunting ridge above all the surrounding elevations, looking down upon the rest of the world, which seemed to be crouching at our feet.

Long before we reached the summit we were saluted by a new bird voice--one that had not been heard farther down the mountain. It was a cordial chirp, which seemed to bid us welcome to the alpine region and to assure us that there was no risk in climbing to these sky-aspiring summits. A glance proved that our little salutarian was the brown-capped rosy finch, which I had not seen since my ascent of Pikes Peak. Down in the green, copsy valley at the base of the mountain we had met with the white-crowned sparrows and Wilson and Audubon warblers; then, as we began to climb the steep shoulder of the mountain, the American pipits had become our comrades, accompanying us about half way up the elevation; now all other birds had disappeared and we entered the arctic precincts of the leucostictes, which, like a gallant bodyguard, escorted us to the summit, cheering us on with their friendly chirping. The bailiwicks of the pipits and the rosy finches slightly overlapped, as did also those of the pipits and the white-crowned sparrows near the great mountain's base. However, no pipits ventured to the upper story of this elevated region--at least, not at the time of our visit, although they may have ascended to the summit later in the season.

How blithe and cheerful were the pretty leucostictes! Now they darted fearlessly about in the air over the summit and the gorges; now they alighted on the wall of the dilapidated old signal station, and anon hopped and flitted about over the extensive snow beds, picking up dainties that were evidently to their taste, all the while beguiling the time with their companionable, half-musical chirping. So far as I observed, they have no real song. If they have, it is strange that they did not furnish a sample of their lyrical gifts on so calm and sweet a summer day in the season of courtship.

What billsome morsels did they find on the snow? We examined their white tablecloth and found a number of small beetles and other insects creeping up through it or crawling around over its surface. Thus Nature spreads her banquet everywhere for her feathered children.

One cannot help falling into the speculative mood as one reflects on these little birds and their remarkable habits. Why do they, of all birds, choose the highest mountain peaks for their summer homes? Might the cause be physiological? Are their lungs, muscles, and nervous systems so constructed as to be adapted to a dry, rare, crisp atmosphere, which would prove injurious, perhaps fatal, to birds of a different structural organization? Who can tell? At all events, they live on these towering elevations all summer long, woo their plainly-clad mates, build their nests, and rear their happy families.

Their nests are set amid the rocks, and are quite bulky, the walls composed of grasses and the lining consisting of soft feathers. In order to procure the grasses required, they must descend at least to the belt of scant vegetation just below the region of bare rocks and boulders. Where they get the downy feathers for the carpet of their nurseries I have not been able to ascertain. No nest has yet been discovered below an elevation of 12,000 feet. Our little bird may, indeed, be called a "haunter of the sky." The height of the breeding season is in the latter part of July. The broods having left the nests, old and young gather in small flocks and range over the peaks and ridges, feeding on the insects to be found on the fields of snow.

No less interesting are the habits of these birds in winter. In October and November most of them descend only to the timber line, where they remain throughout the winter, save as they are driven down into the denser forests by the fierce tempests of this arctic region. What feathered Vikings they are! They do not even make for themselves snow huts for protection from the winter storms. However, a few descend almost to the base of the foothills, while others--perhaps the less hardy--seek a blander climate in the northern part of Mexico.

There are in North America four other species of the genus Leucosticte; the Aleutian, whose habitat is the Aleutian and Prybilof islands and east as far as the island of Kadiak; the gray-crowned, which breeds in British America near the Rocky Mountains, comes to Colorado in winter, and has been taken as far east as western

Iowa; the Hepburn, dwelling chiefly in the mountain ranges of the Pacific coast, breeding mostly in the far North, and in winter coming as far south and east as Nevada and Colorado; and, lastly, the black leucosticte, which winters in the central latitudes in the Rocky Mountains and whose summer range and breeding home is unknown to men of science.

HAPPENINGS BY THE WAY

If one were to keep on writing monographs of all our interesting avian species, the books that would result would make a good-sized library. The few examples that have been given will illustrate what can be done in this direction with the help of the field glass and the handbook. A few chapters will now be given on what might be called "odds and ends of bird life," and these are written not only for the information they may impart, but also for the purpose of showing how many interesting facts can be gathered along the way by the method of bird study commended in our opening chapter.

The prince of American ornithologists, Dr. Elliott Coues, has somewhere said that he would travel a long distance to discover a new kind of bird, or even to ascertain a new fact about a familiar species. I would applaud and echo that sentiment, for by all means let us have bird news that really is news, instead of revamping the familiar facts again and again, as some amateurish writers do. While I am not able to add any new species to science, I have made note of many pleasing incidents in the bird realm, and these, I venture to hope, may be of not a little general interest.

Eastern Phoebe

There is the companionable white-breasted nuthatch which goes scudding up and down the tree trunks with as much ease and aplomb as a fly gliding over a window-pane. I have already told you something about him. I had long been aware that he wedged grains of corn, sunflower seeds, and kernels of nuts in the crannies of the bark; but one day he invented a trick that was a surprise to me. It occurred at a summer resort in northern Indiana, where I noticed a nuthatch hitching up and down and around the slender stem of a sapling, pausing at intervals to thrust something into the crevices of the bark. My curiosity led me to pry into the bird's affairs. Stepping smartly forward, I drove him away, not heeding his vigorous protest of "yank, yank," and examined the bark of the sapling. What did I discover? A colony of black ants were scuttling up and down the tree, apparently under stress of great excitement; and good reason they had, for here and there one of their number was tightly wedged into a chink of the bark, often doubled up into a bow or an angle. They were not killed, at least not all of them, for they were still wiggling their legs and antennas; but they were evidently benumbed, or some of their backs were broken, and they were fastened so securely in the fissures that they could not escape. Does it not look as if the forehanded nuthatch was laying by a supply of ants for a coming time of hunger?

One day a family of wood pewees visited the dooryard of my tent. A multitude of gnats circling about in the air, seemed to be precisely to the taste of the pewee parents and their hungry bairns. The bantlings sat chirping in the saplings, or flitted from twig to twig, twinkling their wings in the coaxing way that is characteristic of young birds, while the papa and mamma swung out into the air, nabbed the insects on the wing, and flew back to the trees, describing many circles, ellipses, and festoons of rare grace and beauty. The snapping of their mandibles could often be heard as they closed upon the fated insects. Most of the gnats thus captured were thrust into the mouths of the young birds, the parents dashing up to them and feeding them without alighting. As lavish a minstrel as the pewee pater familias is under most circumstances, that morning he was too busy to tune his wind harp.

Speaking of the voracious appetites of birds, as exhibited by the young pewees, which never seemed to get enough, I am reminded of something I witnessed one day in a deep, wooded hollow. A red-eyed vireo suddenly appeared in the branches above me, holding an immense green worm in his beak. Then followed a tussle for the "upper hand" that was worth seeing. The bird, holding its squirming victim by one end, proceeded to beat it against the limb, though it was almost too big and recalcitrant for him to handle. Presently the vireo, after a good deal of effort, succeeded in passing his quarry through his bill from end to end, thus reducing it to somewhat smaller dimensions. Still, it was a large morsel for so small a diner.

However, there were some intimations that the bird intended to bolt the worm whole. And that was just what he was planning to do! What a struggle ensued! I would have wagered that the little gourmand had reckoned without his host when he undertook to swallow that immense worm. He twisted his neck this way and that, gulped and squeezed and pried, until I feared he would burst his throat open. At length the worm was partly bolted, but it seemed to stick fast, and the bird stood there with his mandibles pressed far apart, the end of his dinner bulging out of his mouth, and I felt uneasy for a time lest he should choke to death before my very eyes. But, after resting a minute, he gave his neck a number of convulsive twists, and at last succeeded in forcing the unwilling worm down his throat, after which he wiped his bill on the limb with a self-satisfied air and flitted away as happy as a lark, knowing that his faithful craw would do the rest.

A slate-colored junco did a pretty thing in the woods one day of early spring--much more pleasing to see than the incident just described. He had rinsed his feathers in a pool of the little stream down in the hollow, and now he was squatting flat on his belly on the ground in a soft bed of brown leaves, preening and primping his plumes with his little white, conical bill. Now he gave his quills a deft touch, now the feathers of his wing, now those of his dainty breast. Lying there in the sun he presented a perfect picture of feathery laziness. Many a bird I have seen arranging his toilet after a bath while perching on a limb or a twig, and even, as in the case of the brown creeper, while clinging to the bole of a tree, but never before did I see one doing this while lolling on the ground. He was not sick or hurt, simply lazy; for when I went near him he flew away as chipper as a bird could be.

The rambler not only sees many of these pretty bird ways, but he sometimes has a hearty laugh at the birds' expense. During one of my outings a blustering whirlwind started on the summit of a small hill scantily covered with scrub oak. It seized the dead leaves and twirled them about as if in a spasm of anger; then it went scurrying noisily down the steep incline, flinging itself against a couple of large brush heaps in the hollow where a number of fox and Harris sparrows were concealed. They had imagined themselves safe in their brushy covert. Suddenly the whirlwind struck their hiding place with a clang and clatter, sending the birds in a wild panic in every direction. They did not seem to know what had struck them, and, as the wanton breezes tossed them this way and that, they expressed their astonishment in loud and frightened chirping. All over and no harm done, the bird lover burst into a peal of laughter at the discomfiture of his feathered neighbors, who looked at him as if they did not know what to make of his untimely hilarity.

Then, too, one cannot be an observing rambler without stumbling upon some exceedingly odd avian pranks, as the following description will indicate: One day I was sitting on the steep bank of a wooded ravine watching several rare little birds, hoping to discover some of their nests. Presently the susurrus of the hummingbird was heard, and a moment later two ruby-throats, a male and a female, flashed into view on the slope below me. The tiny madam settled on a twig near the ground, while her ruby-throated spouse performed one of the queerest antics I have ever witnessed in featherland. He began to swing back and forth in an arc of almost half a circle, the diameter of which was at least twelve feet, just grazing his mate whenever he reached the lowest point of his concentric movements. Back and forth he swung at least a dozen times, looking like a tiny pendulum moving in an immense arc, and, oddly enough, the segment seemed to be perfectly formed every time. Had the bird wheeled entirely around, he would, I feel sure, have described a circle and not an ellipse. The movement was exceedingly swift, and might well have been called the embodiment of grace. Suddenly, as the diminutive acrobat reached the highest point of his arc, he dashed off to the right in a straight line, followed by his mate, and in a moment both had disappeared. Whether other observers have been witnesses of this curious gambol, I am unable to say.

Have you ever been ill-mannered enough to watch the birds going to bed? I remember spending an evening in the woods playing the role of Paul Pry on my feathered neighbors. The sun was just sinking behind the bluffs on the other side of a broad river--the Missouri--and the moon, which was half full, was hanging high in the blue sky. What were those two large black objects over yonder in the woods? My glass soon revealed their identity--a pair of turkey buzzards perched side by side on a limb, one of them squatted flat on his belly ready to take his first nap. My curiosity led me to go near them, when they spread their broad, sable wings, flew a few rods, and alighted on another horizontal bar. There they sat as long as I could see them in the thickening darkness, turning their heads now and then to see whether their ill-bred visitor was still spying upon them. They made no efforts to conceal themselves, as the small birds do in roosting, for they knew, no doubt, that nothing would carry off fowls of their size.

A little later on the same evening a whip-poor-will darted up from the roadside and flew into the woods a short distance, alighting on a white flag of good size, so that I could plainly see his dark form in the moonlight. Then I was witness of this uncanny bird's table manners, which were entirely unknown to me and may be to others. At irregular intervals he leaped into the air, now in one direction, now in another, captured an insect, and flew back to the top of the flag. Some of his evolutions were quite wonderful, and all of them were the perfection of grace. He described all kinds of curves and loops. On alighting he uttered a low, hollow chuck suggestive of the sepulchral. Another notch had to be cut in the tally-stick of my ornithological journey--I had learned how the whip-poor-will takes his nocturnal dinner of moths and beetles, and I felt that there was still such a thing as news to be gathered in birdland.

Most birds, however, do not take their dinner at night, and therefore it is easier to watch them at their table d'hote. One day a red-headed woodpecker was giving a strapping youngster as large as herself his noonday meal. She came close to him with a morsel in her long bill, and, after pounding it awhile against a limb, she thrust it into the screaming youngling's mouth. But she had failed to reduce it to a swallowable size; it stuck in his throat, and, do what he would, he could not bolt it. It was so large that he was choking; what should be done? The simplest thing you can conceive. The mother bird reached over and impatiently jerked the refractory morsel out of her baby's throat, thumped it vigorously several times against the branch, then gave it to him again, as much as to say, "Now try it! I guess you can manage it this time." And he did, for down his gullet it went with very little effort. Then she went after more provender for his spacious craw. Whenever she came with a tidbit, she would first drop it into a kind of pocket in the bark, and pound it a while to reduce it to a proper consistency; the while the youngster would sit near and watch her with hungry eyes, and often scream in his coaxing way and twinkle his wings, until she was ready to deliver up the tempting fragment.

Once, after she had given him all she had brought, he still opened his mouth and whimpered for more. At this exhibition of gluttony she lost her patience. Would he never be satisfied, the great, greedy, overgrown lubber? He was simply making a slave and a drudge of her. She looked at him for a moment with a savage glitter in her dark eyes, then began to peck him angrily right in the mouth, and drove him peremptorily backward down the limb. Mother patience has its limitations in the bird world as well as elsewhere.

On the same day a bank swallow was feeding her little ones, a half dozen or so, which were ranged on a willow stem at the margin of the river. Every time she flew toward them they set up a vigorous calling to be fed. She procured her food by skimming airily over the river and catching the insects that rose from its surface. Having nabbed one, she would dart with it to her little family, and, without alighting, and scarcely pausing in her swift flight, would thrust it into the mouth of one of the birdkins. Thus she fed them one by one until she had gone the round of the little circle, though sometimes, oddly enough, she would serve the same infant twice in succession.

The little family, all perched in a row, looked very attractive, and I was watching them closely most of the time. Suddenly the mother bird disappeared, and was gone for several minutes. I forgot to keep my eye steadily on the youngsters sitting six in a row, and, to my great surprise, when she reappeared they had left their perch, which was in plain sight, and I could not rediscover them for some time. Finally, however, I espied them cuddling among some leafy twigs a few feet away, where the mother resumed her duties of purveyor. My opinion is that she had begun to feel uneasy for their safety in the exposed place where I could see them so plainly, and so, while I was looking elsewhere, had persuaded them to shift their position. Now they were partly screened by the intervening leaves, and she felt that they were secure.

There can be no doubt that birds have a language which the youngsters soon come to understand, however simple and inarticulated it may be. In a shady hollow, one day of early spring, a pair of tufted titmice were supplying the wants of a family of famishing children, and I invited myself to the family reunion. The young birds had left the nest and were perched in a leafy tree. Most of the time they kept up a great clamor for food--or, perhaps, they shrieked merely from force of habit; but every few minutes one of the parent birds would utter a shrill, commanding cry, at which all the noisy clamorings of the youthful family would suddenly cease, and for a few moments perfect quiet would reign in titmouse town; then the hubbub would begin again, and continue until another order for perfect silence was given. So far as I could see, there was no danger from raptorial foes at hand, but the little family seemed to be in training against the approach of a marauder.

It may be a far cry, but from green-robed spring fancy yourself suddenly flung into the lap of snow-bound winter, to look upon scenes quite different from the foregoing. The Frost King had been playing a good many pranks for a week or two, and once, in a spasm of frigid ill humor, had jammed the mercury in our thermometers a dozen or more degrees below zero, and had held it there quite too long for our comfort. More than once had he shrieked and blustered and stamped his feet incontinently, and more than once sent his legions of wind, sleet, and snow howling through the leafless woods. Everybody in our central latitudes knows what an explosive old fellow the Frost King is, and how fierce and savage he can become let the mood once seize him.

Sometimes, too, by the hour he had ground his ice crystals to powder in mid-air and hurled them to the earth, covering its surface with a robe of purest white, thus proving that, with all his rudeness and bluster, he is an old gentleman of aesthetic tastes. One evening his mood became blander, and he dropped his crystals from the sky in large, damp flakes, which clung tenaciously to the branches and twigs; then during the night his breath became chilled and froze the snowy cylinders, and when morning broke the woods were a miracle of loveliness, every leaf and twig bearing a ridge of gleaming pearls, while the sylvan floor was pure white. Soon the sun was shining from an unmarred sky, and the snow-clad earth smiled back in shimmering recognition. It was a day for worship in God's first sanctuary.

Yet it was a day for watching the gambols of the birds, and such occupation by no means interfered with the spirit of worship. In the depths of the woods the white-breasted nuthatches were holding a friendly interview. How affectionately they talked to one another in idioms all their own, saying "Hick! hick!" and "Yank! yank!" and "Ha-ha! ha-ha! ha-ha!" which may mean anything that is kind and cordial and confidential. They were either playing at a game of tag, or were having a peep-show among the bushes, hiding for a moment in some leafy cluster, then dashing in pursuit of one another in the most frolicksome way. I crept in under the arches of the snow-clad bushes to watch their caperings more closely, but the birds at once quieted down, and went about their more prosaic vocation of grub gathering. They were no doubt "aching" to frisk about among the snowy bushes, but would not indulge their playful mood under the eye of a human spectator.

Presently one of them was seen carefully primping his feathers--a function that I had not previously seen a nuthatch perform. His plumes seemed to be really quite damp, and, as there was no water at hand--the streams being mailed with ice as well as nearly a half mile away--he must have used a snowbank for his lavatory. But you ask how he arranged his toilet. I had several times seen the little brown creeper clinging to the vertical wall of a tree and preening his plumes after a bath, and it was natural to suppose that his congener, the nuthatch, being also a bird of reptatory habits, would follow the same formula. But not so! Instead of clinging to the upright bole of a tree, Master Nuthatch perched crosswise on a twig like a robin or a chickadee, and smoothed his ruffled plumes.

After this interesting interview with the nuthatches, I trudged about in the woods for some time without seeing any birds. What had become of my feathered neighbors, my companions in every ramble throughout the winter? Had the storm driven them to other climes where bland winds prevailed? Oh, no! See what prudent creatures they were that wintry day. At the eastern border of the woods, where the sun shone warmly and the keen westerly breeze was broken and tempered, my little friends were found in goodly numbers, well knowing where the Frost King's anger would be softened.

Here were nuthatches and chickadees in plenty, and also tufted tits, tree sparrows, juncos, downy woodpeckers, and, to make the complement as nearly full as possible, a hairy woodpecker drummed and chir-r-r-red, several blue jays complained in the distance, and a goldfinch swinging overhead threaded the air with festoons of black and gold. And here I witnessed a new and pretty antic of a tree sparrow, which flew over from a cornfield hard by and perched on a dogwood sapling only a few feet away; then it plunged its beak into the little snowbank on the twig before it and ate greedily of the snow, some of the crystals clinging to its mandibles, just as the crumbs adhere to the lips of a hungry boy. Had the exclamation not been so much like slang, I would have cried "Next!" And there was a "next," as sure as you live, for the little bird soon flitted to another twig in the same tree and, reaching up, daintily sipped from the dripping underside of the branch just above and in front of it. Its thirst having been assuaged, it flew over into the adjoining field to resume its winter feast of seeds and berries.

And what was happening over in the field? Something worth noting, to be sure. A coterie of juncos and tree sparrows were breakfasting on the seeds of a clump of tall weeds, a few of the little feasters perched on the swaying stems, while others stood on the snow on the ground and picked the seeds from the racemes that were bent down by their burden of crystals. When I went to the place, I could see the delicate tracery of their feet on the snow, as if they had been writing their autographs on an untarnished scroll. Two tiny footprints at regular intervals, one a little before the other, and each pair connected with the next by a slender thread or two traced by the bird's claws--that is a junco's or a tree sparrow's trail in the snow.

A little later a scattering flock of tree sparrows were skipping about on the snowy floor of the woods, picking up at quick intervals a palatable tidbit. Birds often find edibles on the surface of the snow when our duller eyes can see nothing but immaculate whiteness. What long leaps the little birds took across the snow, which looked like a marble pavement with fairies dancing upon it! Near by, on one of the lower twigs of a thorn bush, a sparrow sat with feathers fluffed up and wings hanging negligently at his side, as if he were taking a siesta after a hearty meal of weed seeds and winter berries. Two of his companions soon joined him in his noonday rest, the trio making a pretty picture sitting there within an inch or two of the ground.

It was not very long before a tree sparrow perpetrated another surprise, proving that this species is not without character, as indeed no species is. He leaped to the bole of a sapling, clinging there a few moments like a chickadee or a wren, while he pecked an appetizing morsel from the bark; then he dropped down to the snow for a brief breathing spell, after which he sprang up again to the sapling for a few more bits, repeating the little performance a number of times.

In the same part of the woods a company of chickadees was flitting about in the trees, plunging into the little snowbanks on the twigs, sometimes standing in them up to their white bosoms, and often brushing a segment to the ground, thus making numerous breaches in the white drifts. The racket they made with their scolding and piping might have been called a musical din. Deciding to watch them a while, I flung myself down upon the snow. This act was the signal for a precious to-do among the nervous little potherers. Did any one ever hear or read of such a performance in all the annals of birdland? What in the world did it mean--a man lying flat on the ground out there in the woods? I was highly amused at the hurly-burly, and decided to add still more variety to it. Suddenly I sprang to my feet with a shout. Several of the birds dropped, as if shot, into a thorn bush below them, where they set up a hubbub that would have made on old-time Puritan laugh, even at the risk of being censured for levity. By and by they quieted down, and one of them began to whistle his pretty minor tune with as much serenity as if he had never been excited in his life. My winter outing proved that the Frost King and the hardy birds often go cheek by jowl, as if they were on terms of the most cordial fraternity.

ODDS AND ENDS

The ornithologist is always interested in noting how the conduct of birds of the same species differs and agrees in different localities. In a previous chapter some of the differences between the avifauna of Ohio and Kansas have been described, but a good deal still remains to be said, teaching more than one lesson in comparative ornithology.

At the beginning of my studies in the Sunflower state the song sparrows proposed an enigma for my solution, whether wittingly or unwittingly, I know not. In Ohio they were the most lavish singers in the outdoor chorus, chanting their sweet lays every month in the year, summer or winter; indeed, their most vigorous recitals were often given in February and March, when there was dearth of other bird music.

But what about the song sparrows of Kansas? The first winter and spring passed, and yet my numerous rambles in their haunts did not bring to my waiting ear one first-class song sparrow concert. A few feeble, half-hearted wisps of melody on days that were especially mild were the only vocal performances they vouchsafed. To put it bluntly and truthfully, I never, during my residence of five and a half years in Kansas, heard a first-rate song sparrow trill. Nor is that all. In the Buckeye state these birds were disposed to be sociable, often selecting their dwellings near our suburban homes, visiting our dooryards, singing their blithe roundels on the ridge of the barn roof or a post of the garden fence. Not only so, but their songs were often heard in some of the principal streets of towns where trees were abundant.

Song Sparrow

Quite otherwise was the conduct of their western cousins, which seldom came to town or even near a human residence in the country, but kept themselves ensconced in the matted copses in the banks of the Missouri River or in the deep hollows running back from the broad valley. In these sequestered haunts they were quite wary, usually scuttling out of sight at my approach. True, in Ohio many individuals also chose out-of-the-way places for habitats, but even then they were not timid, for often they would mount to the top of a bush or a sapling in plain sight and trill sweetly by the hour, with never a quaver of fear. At rare intervals a Kansas sparrow would visit the thicket on the vacant lot near my house, but, my! how shy he was! And as for singing, he would only squeak a little score.

Wondering at the reticence of the Kansas sparrows, I wrote to a friend living in Springfield, Ohio, my former home, and inquired what the song sparrows were doing in that locality. His reply was that, as usual, they had been singing with splendid effect on almost every day after the middle of February. What is the reason of this difference between the eastern and western birds? They are, according to the systematists, the same type, and yet they behave so differently. The solution of the problem is, after all, quite simple. In Kansas the song sparrows are winter residents exclusively, passing farther north when the breeding season approaches; only at rare intervals does a pair decide to remain in the state throughout the summer; whereas in the Buckeye state these birds are permanent residents, remaining throughout the year, and therefore they feel sufficiently at home to tune their lyres at all seasons. On the other hand, being only winter visitors in Kansas, they do not seem to be able to overcome their shyness; either that, or their wind harps are out of tune. As a matter of fact, migrating birds seldom sing a great deal in their winter homes, their best lyrical efforts being husbanded for their breeding haunts. I once spent part of the month of June in Minnesota, almost directly north of my Kansas field of research, and there found these charming minstrels as tuneful and affable as the most exacting bird lover could wish. Perhaps some of the very sparrows that spend the winter in silence in northeastern Kansas trill their finest arias in their summer homes on the shores of Lake Minnetonka or in the boggy hollows in the neighborhood of Duluth.

When I first began to plan for moving back to Ohio, I was foolish enough to fear that the song sparrows of that state might have changed their habits during the years of my absence, and that I should be disappointed in them: but no need of borrowing trouble on their account, for they were the same blithe and familiar birds, trilling their sweetest chansons in the trees in the residence portion of the town in which I lived. And sing! Were there ever birds with more dulcet tones, with finer voice register, or with a greater variety of tunes in their repertoire?

Going back to Kansas in winter, we note that the song sparrows, instead of remaining at one place, shifted about a good deal more than I had ever known them to do in the East. In December a pair found a dwelling in the weed clumps and brush heaps of a hollow a short distance from the Missouri River; but they soon deserted this spot, well sheltered as it was, none being seen there until the twenty-third of February. It surprised me to find another pair, and sometimes two pairs, in a thicket right on the bank of the wide river, where they were exposed to many of the winter blasts, especially those that swept down from the frozen north. Up in the deep, winding ravine they might have had excellent shelter and, so far as I could see, just as good feeding. However, I have long ago learned that there is no accounting for tastes in the bird realm any more than in the human realm.

The hardiest of the Mniotiltidae tribe are the myrtle warblers, which dapple the whitened edges of winter, both autumn and spring, with their golden rumps and amber brooches. Evidently these birds are shyer of the rigorous Ohio winters than of the more mild-mannered Kansas weather. In the former state I never saw a myrtle warbler after the first or second week in November, while in Kansas I came upon a flock of them in a wooded hollow by the river on the eighth of December, 1897, and then after a severe snowstorm had swept over the region from the western prairies. It seemed odd to find these dainty featherland blossoms when the whole country was covered with an ermine of snow.

Then they disappeared, and I did not expect to see them again until the next spring; but on the fourteenth of February, which was a warm, vernal day thrust into the midst of winter, a flock of perhaps a dozen were flitting and chirping among the trees in the suburbs of the city, their hoarse little chep, always giving one the impression that the birds have taken a cold which has affected their vocal cords, sounding as familiar as of old. However, that very evening at dusk a black cloud, charged with electricity and bellowing with anger, came up out of the west like a young Lochinvar, and hurled a fierce storm across the hills and valleys, and the next day not a myrtle warbler was to be seen in all the countryside, though I tramped weary miles in search of them. The tempest had doubtless frightened them away to the suaver southland, from which they did not return until the following spring.

One of my most pleasing observations was made on December 19, 1902. There had been a number of days of severe weather, accompanied by hard storms. Six inches of snow lay on the ground. Now the storm had spent its force, the sun was shining genially, and the snow was melting. Warm as it was, I was greatly surprised to find a flock of myrtle warblers in the woods so late in the season. They had braved the storms of the preceding week, and were as chipper and active as myrtle warblers could be. But their employment was a still greater surprise. They were darting about in the air among the treetops, as well as amid the bushes in the deep ravine, catching insects on the wing. That insects should be flying after the wintry weather of the previous week was still more surprising than that the warblers should be here to dine upon them. Soon after that day, however, the little yellow-rumps must have taken the wing route to a more genial climate, for they were seen no more that winter.

Of a more permanent character was the residence of the jolly juncos, which dwelt all winter in northeastern Kansas, let the weather be never so lowering. Always active and alert, flitting from bush to weed, and from the snow-carpeted ground to the gnarled oak saplings, now pilfering a dinner of wild berries and now a luncheon of weed seeds, they seemed to generate enough warmth in their trig little bodies to defy old Boreas to do his best. Water flowing from melting snow must be ice-cold, yet the juncos plunged into the crystal pools and rinsed their plumes with as much apparent relish as if their lavatory were tepid instead of icy, and as if balmy instead of nipping winds were blowing.

One day I watched a member of this family taking his dinner of wild grapes. Finding a dark red cluster, he would pick off the juiciest berry he could reach, press it daintily between his white mandibles for a few moments, swallow a part of the pulp, and drop the rest to the ground. What part of the grape did he eat? That is the precise problem I could not solve with certainty, for on examining the rejected portions that had been flung to the ground I found that one seed still remained, together with part of the pulp and all of the broken rind. I half suspect, though, that Master Junco likes to tipple a little--never enough, however, be it remembered, to make him reel or lose his senses. No! no! a toper Master Junco is not; he is too sane a bird for that! Would that all the citizens of our republic would display as much sound judgment and self-control.

Where all the birds sleep on biting winter nights it would be difficult to say, but the acute little juncos lease the farmer's corn shocks hard by the woods. At dusk you may startle a dozen of them from a single shock. They dart pellmell from their hiding places, chippering their protest, and when you examine the shock you find cozy nooks and ingles among the leaves and stalks, where they find couches and at the same time coverts from the sharp winds. As you stand at the border of the woods in the gloaming you can hear the rustling of the fodder as the juncos move about in their tepees, trying to find the choicest and snuggest berths. Usually they select the tops of the standing shocks, perhaps for safety; yet some may be found also in the shocks that have partly fallen to the ground.

In the latter part of February the juncos began to rehearse their spring songs, which were a welcome sound in the almost unbroken silence of the winter. The nearer the spring approached, the higher they mounted in the trees, and the more prolonged was their flight, as if they were practicing their wing exercises to inure their muscles to the strain that would be put upon them when they undertook their long journey to their northern summer homes; for, of course, the juncos do not breed in our central latitudes, but hie to the northern part of the United States and the Dominion of Canada.

In Ohio the brown creepers and the golden-crowned kinglets were constant winter companions in the woods; but, although Kansas is considerably farther south, they do not seem to be winter residents there--at least, not in the northeastern part of the state--the only exception being that in January, 1903, several creepers were observed in my yard. One may well wonder why these birds are winter residents in Ohio and only migrants in a latitude that is two degrees farther south.

There was some scant compensation in the presence of the winter wren one winter in the Sunflower state. The fourteenth of December brought one of these brown Lilliputians to a deep hollow in town, where he chattered petulantly and scampered along an old paling fence. No more winter wrens were seen until January seventh, when one darted out of some bushes on the bank of a stream about two miles south of town. My next jaunt to this hollow took place on the twenty-seventh, when, to my surprise, a hermit thrush was seen in a clump of bushes and saplings--a bird that I supposed had been sunning himself for at least a month in the genial South. While tramping about trying to get another view of the unconventional thrush, I frightened a winter wren from a cluster of weeds and bushes. My! how alarmed he was! Uttering a loud chirp, he darted down to the center of the stream and slipped into a little cave formed by ice and snow frozen over a clump of low bushes. There he hid himself like an Eskimo in his snow hut. My trudging near by frightened the bird out of the farther doorway, and he dashed away pellmell, hurling a saucy gird of protestation at me, and was seen by me no more. I examined the little snow house. It was very cunning indeed, and might well have made a cozy shelter for the little wren in stormy weather. My next meeting with a winter wren occurred on the fifteenth of February, in the same hollow, but about an eighth of a mile nearer the river. A query arises here: Did I see four different winter wrens during the winter, or only one in four different localities? Who can tell?

That is not all about the winter wrens. My first winter in Kansas was the severest I experienced in that state; yet it was the only winter of the five I spent in Kansas that brought me the winter wren. If it would do any good, one might ask again the question why. Although the winter wren is a migrant in Ohio, as he is for the most part in northeastern Kansas, yet I never heard his song in the former state, while in the latter I was fortunate enough to listen to his tinkling melody three times the first spring I spent there. After that I never heard him, and indeed saw him only a few times. But the sweet, silvery roulade--could there be anything more charming in the world of outdoor music?

My winter rambles--and winter is almost as good a time for bird study as summer-- enabled me to note some variety of temperament in the avian realm. One thing we soon learn in our winter outings: Few birds are recluses. No, they are sociable creatures, living in what might be called nomadic communities. In the spring-time, during the mating season, they pair off and become more or less exclusive and secretive, keeping close to the precincts they have selected; but in winter they grow more neighborly, and move about in the woods or over the fields in flocks of various sizes.

The woodland flocks usually consist of a number of species all of which seem to be on the most cordial terms, having, no doubt, a community of interest. As we quietly pursue our way in this wooded vale, we see no birds for some distance. Presently a fine, protesting "chick-a-dee-dee! chick-a-dee-dee!" breaks the silence. It is the warning call of the tomtit or chickadee, which we soon espy tilting about on his trapeze of twigs in the trees or bushes. But you may depend upon it he is not alone; he is only a part of the rim of a feathered colony dwelling near at hand, and consisting, very likely, of tufted titmice, white-breasted nuthatches, juncos, tree sparrows, blue jays, one or two downy woodpeckers, a pair of cardinals, a flicker or two, and a cackling red-breasted woodpecker. There may be even a song sparrow in the company and a couple of brown creepers, and possibly a flock of purple finches, chirping cheerily in the tops of the trees.

While, in the spring and summer, birds are to be found in nearly every part of the woods, never many at one place, the opposite condition prevails in the winter. Sometimes you may walk almost a half mile without seeing or hearing a single bird;

then you suddenly come upon a good-sized company of them, somewhat scattered, it is true, but within easy hailing distance. Nor do they always remain in the same localities, but move about, now here, now there, like nomads looking for the best foraging places. For instance, on the first of January, after leaving the city, I saw not a bird until I reached a pleasant sylvan hollow at least a half mile away. Here a merry crowd greeted the pedestrian. It was composed of all the birds I have just named, with flocks of bluebirds and goldfinches thrown in for good measure. On the fourteenth of January a company--either the same or another--was found in a small copsy hollow only a quarter of a mile from the city, while the spot previously occupied was deserted. It is pleasant to think of these feathered troopers roaming about the country in search of Nature's choicest storehouses. The code that obtains in these movable birdvilles is this, as near as I am able to analyze it: Each one for himself, and yet all for one another.

The familiar adage, "Birds of a feather flock together," is not always true, for in winter birds of many a feather often flock together. It may be asked, Why? No doubt largely for social ends. Nothing is more evident to the observer than that most birds love company, and a good deal of it. Their genial conversation among themselves as they pursue their work and play fully proves that. Another object is undoubtedly protection. Birds have enemies, many of them, and when the woods are bare there is little chance for hiding, and so they must be especially on the alert. Let a hawk come gliding silently and slyly down the vale, and before he gets too near some keen little eye espies him, the alarm is sounded, and the whole company scurries into the thickets or trees for safety. The chickadees and titmice seem to be a sort of sentry for the company.

A large part of the time in birdland is spent in solving the "bread-and-butter" problem. And how do our feathered citizens solve this important problem in the cold weather? Nature has spread many a banquet for her avian children, although they must usually rustle for their food just as we must in the human world. The nuthatches, titmice, woodpeckers, and brown creepers find larvae, grubs, borers, and insects' eggs in the crannies of the bark and other nooks and niches; the goldfinches find something to their taste in the buds of the trees and also make many a meal of thistle and sunflower seeds; the juncos and tree sparrows, forming a joint stock company in winter, rifle all kinds of weeds of their seedy treasures; the blue jays lunch on acorns and berries when they cannot find enough juicy grubs to satisfy their appetites, and so on through the whole list.

By playing the spy on the birds we may learn much about their dietary habits. It is the first of January, and we are in a wooded hollow. There is a tufted titmouse; now he flits to the ground, picks up a tidbit, darts up to a twig, places his morsel under his claws, and proceeds to peck it to pieces. Our binocular shows that it is something yellow, but we cannot make out what it is. As we draw near, the bird seizes the fragment with his bill--perhaps he fears we will filch it from him--and flits about among the bushes on the steep bank, looking for a place to stow his "goody." Presently he pushes it into a crevice of the bark, hammers it tightly into place, and darts away with a merry chirp. We go to the spot and find that his hidden treasure is a grain of corn which he has purloined from the farmer's field on the slope. A few minutes later another tit--or the same one--slyly thrusts a morsel in among some leaves and twigs on the bank, even pulling the leaves down over it for a screen. It turns out to be a small acorn. That is one of Master Tit's ways--storing away provisions for a time of need. With his stout, conical beak he is able to break the shell of an acorn, peck a corn grain into swallowable bits, and tear open the toughest casing of a cocoon. He will even break the hard pits of the dogwood berry to secure the kernel within, the ground below often being strewn with the shell fragments. No danger of Parus bicolor coming to want or going to the poorhouse.

Another day the juncos are feeding on the seeds of the foxtail or pigeon grass, in an old orchard hard by the border of the woods. Sometimes they will make a dinner of berries--the kinds too that are regarded as poisonous to man--eating the juicy pulp in their dainty way, and dropping the seeds and rind to the ground. In the ravine furrowed out by a stream--this is down in one of the hollows--there is a perfect network of bird tracks in the snow beneath a clump of weed stalks. How dainty they are, like tiny chains, twisted and coiled about on the white surface! They were made by the juncos and tree sparrows, and on examining the seed pods and clusters above the bank we note that they are torn and ragged. The feathered banqueters have been here, and while they were industriously culling the pods, some of the seeds fell to the white carpet below, and these have been carefully picked up by the birds, as we see, so that nothing should be wasted.

It is not often you catch a bird in the singing mood in the winter; yet on December 19, a purple finch was piping quite a vivacious tune in the woods. Of course, he was not in his best voice, but his performance was good enough to entitle it to the name of bird music. The finches, by the way, are strong flyers. At your approach, instead of flitting off a little way, perhaps to the next tree or bush, after the manner of the tits and nuthatches and many other birds, the finches tarry in the tree-tops as long as they deem it safe, then take to wing and fly to a distant part of the woods, and you may not see them again that day. However, they may come back to you after a while, as if they relished your company. The goldfinches are also long-distance flyers, not flitters. Usually they give some signal of their presence, either by their vivacious "pe-chick-o-pe" or their childlike and semi-musical calls; but there are times when a good-sized flock of them will suddenly appear in the tree-tops above you, and you cannot tell when they arrived, for you did not see them there at all a few minutes before.

WAYSIDE OBSERVATIONS

The previous chapter closed with some notes on the behavior of birds in the winter time. My home rambling grounds in northeastern Kansas were extremely undulating, cut up into ridges and ravines, most of which were covered with a thick growth of weeds, bushes, and timber. In some places the thickets were so dense as to be almost impenetrable. This diversity in the topography of the country afforded considerable variety in the faunal life of the region.

For example, in bitter winter weather most of the birds would hug the sheltered hollows, where they found coverts in the copses, and would avoid the hilltops, which were exposed to the nipping winds blowing from the western prairies. As the spring approached, bringing blander weather, they gradually moved up the hillsides, many of them finding billsome seeds and berries on the summits.

However, note a difference in the temperament of individuals of the same species. On the bitterest days of winter I would sometimes leave the sheltered hollows and lowlands and clamber to the summits of the wind-swept hills, and, oddly enough, on the exposed heights I occasionally flushed a solitary bird, which would spring up from the weeds or copses and dart away with a frightened cry. More than likely it would be an individual of the same species as some of the more socially disposed tenants of the lower grounds, but for some reason, what, I know not, it preferred the life of an anchorite; it did not care for society, even of its own kith. Invariably, too, these feathered recluses were extremely shy, scuttling away like frightened deer as I approached their cloistered haunts.

These notes stir several queries in one's mind. Is there such a thing as social ostracism in the bird world? Might these hilltop eremites have committed some crime or some breach of decorum that effected their banishment from respectable avicular society? Or were they simply of a sullen or retiring disposition, choosing seclusion rather than the company of their kind? These questions must be left unanswered. Most frequently the lone bird would be a song sparrow. Once a brilliant cardinal was trying to conceal himself in a clump of bushes and weeds far up the hillside, acting very much like a social outcast. For some reason that he did not see fit to explain he wanted to be alone.

If the song sparrows of eastern Kansas belie their name and seldom fall into the lyrical mood, as has been said, the like cannot be said of the robins, which, in the proper season, were very lavish of their minstrelsy. Their favorite singing time in the West, as in the East, was at the "peep of dawn." How often their ringing carols broke into my early morning dreams!

Have you ever noticed the tentative efforts of the robins in the early spring, at the beginning of the song season, before they get their harps in full tune? It is interesting and amusing to listen to their rehearsals, of which they need quite a number before they acquire full control of their voices. This is the method: Starting off on a tune, they will keep it up until their voices break; then they will stop a while to recover breath, and presently make another attempt with perhaps slightly better success. At first they are able to pipe only a syllable or two before their voices break. After a while they succeed in carrying the tune for a respectable little run, but sooner or later their voices will go all to pieces or slide up into a falsetto, making another pause necessary. By and by, however, after much practice, they gain perfect vocal control, and are able to sustain their songs for a long time without a mishap. When the voice of the rehearsing bird breaks, it apparently runs too high in the scale for the bird's register, just as the voice of a sixteen-year-old boy is apt to do, to his own confusion and the amusement of his friends.

Northern Cardinal

Another fact about robin music may be of interest to those who have not observed it. In the early spring these birds are extremely lyrical, that being their season of courtship; then will follow a few weeks of comparative silence--the time when there are little ones in need of parental care. At this period the husbands, it would seem, are either too busy or too wary to sing a great deal. But now note: When the youngsters have flown from the nest and are able to take care of themselves, the silence in robindom is again broken, and there is a flood-tide of melody from early morning till eventide. The second lyrical period lasts until another nest has been built and another clutch of eggs has been hatched, when the choralists again relapse into comparative silence.

Since coming back to Ohio, I imagine that the eastern robins are better singers than their western relatives. Their voices, to my ear, are clearer and more ringing, less apt to break into a squeak at the top of their register, and there is more variety of expression as well as greater facility in managing the technique. I think this is not all fancy, yet I would not speak with the assurance of the dogmatist.

In the good Jayhawker state the orchard orioles are more abundant than they are in the eastern and northeastern part of the state of Ohio. Indeed, the range of this species is more southerly than that of their congeners, the Baltimore orioles. In their proper latitude no birds, or at least few of them, are more lavish of their melody than the orchard orioles. What a ringing voice the oriole possesses! His song has a saucy note of challenge running through it, and also a human intonation that makes it rarely attractive. All day long the male sings his cheery solos, scarcely pausing for breath or food, now sitting on the topmost twig of a dead apple tree in the orchard, now amid the screening foliage of a maple in the yard, and anon on the other side of the street in a stately cottonwood. But where is that modest little personage, his wife? She is seldom heard, and almost as seldom seen. It is really remarkable--her gift of concealment. When she builds her nest is a mystery. It is often so deftly hidden that you would not be likely to find it in a long hunt. In the spring of 1898 a pair of orchard orioles took up their residence in the trees about my house, the male singing his brisk overtures, the female seen only at flitting intervals and never heard. Watch as I would, I could not surprise her laying the timbers of her cottage, which I felt sure was being built somewhere in the trees. Indeed, I did not discover it until autumn came, long after the orioles, old and young, had taken flight to a balmier clime, and the trees were stripped of their leaves, when, lo! it appeared in plain view on one of the trees on the opposite side of the street, the very place where I had not thought of looking for it.

The Baltimore orioles as a rule are not so secretive; yet during the summer of 1898 a pair of these firebirds led me a fruitless chase. Their secret was not divulged until the leaves had fallen the next autumn, when there the nest hung in the midst of a tall cottonwood in my back yard close to the house. Lord Baltimore and his mate usually suspend their nests on the outer branches of the trees, where they are not hard to discover, but this pair did not follow the common formula, for the nest was placed in the thickest part of the foliage, so that it was impossible to see it from the ground until the branches were bare.

Of all the malaperts of birddom none excel and few equal the white-eyed vireo for volubility and downright audacity. All his songs--and he has quite a respectable list of them--seem to be either a protest or a challenge; a protest against your intrusion into his precincts, a challenge to find him and his nest if you can. Again and again in Kansas I crept into their bushy coverts just for the purpose of receiving a sound scolding. Such a berating did they give me, telling me of all my faults and foibles, that I certainly ought to remain humble all the rest of my days. A half dozen viragoes could not have done better--that is, worse. They would flit about in the bushes above my head, their little white eyes gleaming with fire, and call me all the names they could lay their tongues to. I wonder whether the white-eyes have a dictionary of epithets. Nature has done an odd thing in making the white-eyed vireo.

Their nests are not easy to find, although they do not always make a great deal of effort at concealment. Like all the vireo tribe, they suspend their tiny baskets from the fork or crotch of a horizontal twig. The nest is somewhat bulkier than the compact little cup of the red-eyed vireo, and is apt to be more carefully concealed in the foliage, although I have found more than one nest that was hung in plain sight. I remember one in particular. It was dangling from the outer twigs of a small bush by the side of the woodland path which I was pursuing. In fact, it could be distinctly seen from the path. In spite of the mother's pleadings, protests, and objurgations, I stepped over to inspect her pendant domicile, whose holdings were four baby white-eyes, their eyelids still glued together. As the twigs stirred, they opened their mouths for food, and I decided to accommodate them. Taking a bit of cracker from my haversack, I moistened it, and rolled it into a pellet between my finger and thumb; then, gently swaying the bushes, I induced the bantlings to open their mouths, when I dropped the morsel into one of the tiny throats. You ought to have seen the wry face baby made as it gulped down the new kind of food, which had such an odd taste. It was plain that the callow nestling was able to distinguish this morsel from the palatable diet it had been accustomed to. Possibly it suffered from a temporary fit of indigestion, but no permanent harm was done by my experiment, for when I called on them again a few days later, the birdkins four were safe and well, their eyes open, and their instincts sufficiently developed to cause them to cuddle low in their basket instead of opening their mouths.

Bell's Vireo

The rambler who would hear a real outdoor concert should rise early, swallow a few bits of cracker and a cup of coffee, and seek some bird-haunted hollow or woodland just as day begins to break. One morning I pursued this plan, and was more than compensated for the loss of an hour or two of sleep. Just as the east began to blush I found myself in a favorite wooded hollow.

What a potpourri of bird song greeted my ear! How many choralists took part in the matutinal concert I cannot say, but there were scores of them. The volume of song would sometimes swell to a full-toned orchestra, and then for a few moments it would sink almost to a lull, all of it like the flow and ebb of the tides of a sea of melody. It was interesting to note how several voices would sometimes run into a chime when they struck the same chord.

Let me call the roll of the members of that feathered choir. First, and most gifted of all, were a couple of brown thrashers, whose tones were as strong and sweet as those of a silver cornet, making the echoes ring across the hollow. I have listened to many a thrasher song in the North, the South, and the West, but have never heard a voice of better timbre than that of one of the tawny vocalists singing that morning, as he sat on the topmost twig of an oak tree and flung out his medley upon the morning air. It is wonderful, anyway, with what an ecstasy the thrasher will sometimes sing. Nothing could be plainer than that he sings for the pure pleasure of it--an artist deeply in love with his art.

Falling a little behind the thrashers in vocal power and technical execution were the catbirds, which sent up their cavatinas from the bushes in the hollow. Their voices lacked the volume and strength of their rivals, yet some of their strains were truly the quintessence of sweetness.

Conspicuous members of the early chorus were the wood thrushes, a dozen or more of which were often singing at the same time. From every part of the woods their peals arose. Of course, there was no attempt--at least, so far as I could discover--to sing in concert, but each minstrel followed his own sweet will, and so the combined result was not what you would call a harmony, but a medley, albeit a very pleasing one. If the wood thrush's execution were less labored, he would certainly be a marvelous songster, and even as it is, he furnishes unending delight to those whose ears are trained to appreciate avian minstrelsy.

Two or three rose-breasted grosbeaks piped their liquid, childlike arias; towhees, at least a half-dozen of them, flung forth their loud, explosive trills that have a real musical quality; several cardinals whistled as if they meant to drown out all the other voices; scarlet and summer tanagers drawled their good-natured tunes, while their rich robes gleamed in the level rays of the rising sun; running like silver threads through all the other music, could be heard the fine trills of the field sparrows; the swinging chant of the creeping warblers and the loud rattle of the Tennessee warblers ran high up in the scale, furnishing a gossamer tenor; that golden optimist, the Baltimore oriole, piped his cheery recitative in the tops of the trees; chickadees supplied the minor strains and tufted titmice the alto; four or five turtle doves soothed the ear with their meditative cooing; while the calls and songs of numerous jays and a few yellow-breasted chats made a kind of trombone accompaniment. Surely it is worth one's while to rise early to the haunts of the birds to hear such a tumult of song.

One spring I made up my mind to make a closer study than ever of the dainty creeping warbler, wishing to know just how he contrives to scuttle up and down the boles and branches of the trees with so much ease and grace. He is the only warbler we have in eastern North America that makes a habit of scaling the tree trunks and descending them head downward. How does he do this? The muscles of his legs and pelvis are as elastic as India rubber, so that he can twist and twirl about in a marvelous way, pointing his head one moment to the east and the next, without losing his hold, in the opposite direction. He is able to swing himself around almost as if he were hung on a pivot.

But how does he hold himself on his shaggy wall as he hitches head downward? Just as the nuthatch does--not by keeping both feet directly under him, as most people suppose, but by thrusting one foot slightly forward and the other outward and backward, thus preserving his balance at the same time that he holds himself firmly with his sharp little claws to his upright wall. Some of the pictures of the creeper seen in the books are not quite true to creeper methods of clinging and locomotion, for they represent him as stuck to the bark of a tree trunk with both feet invisible, presumably held directly under his striped breast. In the real position it is likely that one or both feet could be seen, the one thrust forward and the other flung back and to one side. At least one foot would be visible, whatever the angle at which the bird would be inspected, and from many points of view both of his tiny feet may be plainly seen in the position described.

Our little striped friend, usually called in the books the black-and-white warbler, is not, after all, so expert a creeper as is the nuthatch, which may be called the arboreal skater par excellence. The warbler does not go scuttling straight down a vertical bole or branch as the nuthatch does, but swings his lithe body from side to side, as if he did not loosen the hold of both feet simultaneously but alternately. Besides, both in ascending and descending he must have more frequent recourse to his wings to tide him over the difficult places. While the nuthatch can glide over the smoothest and hardest bark, and even descend the wall of a brick house, his sharp claws taking a firm grip on the edges of the bricks, the warbler is not quite so much of a gymnast, for when he strikes a difficult spot in his promenade ground, he flies or flits over it to the next protuberance which his claws can hold. He has a decided advantage, however, over all his warbler kin, for he is not only gifted with the creeping talent, but is also just as dexterous as they in perching on a horizontal twig.

The little bird known as the brown creeper belongs to a different avicular family entirely, but in one respect he is like the black-and-white warbler--that is, he scales the trunks and branches of the trees. There, however, the resemblance ceases, for the creeper rarely goes head downward, evidently thinking that the proper position for a bird's head is pointing toward the sky, not toward the ground. Besides, he seldom, if ever, sits crosswise on a perch; no, he is an inveterate creeper. My study of him proves that he does not hold his feet directly under his breast, but spreads them out well toward either side, knowing instinctively how to make a broad enough base to enable him to preserve his center of gravity.

Like the woodpecker, he uses his stiff tail as a brace; nor does he go zigzagging up his wall after the manner of the creeping warbler, but hitches along in a direct line-- unless, of course, a tidbit attracts him to one side--proving that he is a true creeper, one to the manner born. However, the warbler has one advantage--he is able to perch with perfect security on a twig, an accomplishment that has not yet been attained by his little brown cousin. How cunningly the creeper peeps into the crannies of the bark as he plies his trade, thrusts his long, curved beak into the tiny holes and crevices, and draws out a worm or a grub, which the next moment goes twinkling down his throat! His economic value to the farmer and the fruit grower cannot be estimated, and he should never be destroyed.

The conduct of different birds is not alike upon their arrival from the South at their summer nesting haunts in our more northern latitudes; some heralding their advent with jubilant song as if in greeting to the familiar scenes, while others are silent and wary. The first I knew of the Baltimore and orchard orioles last spring, they were singing blithely in the trees about the house; but the brown thrashers flitted about slyly and silently for a few days, apparently to make sure that the coast was clear of danger; having done which, they burst into their dithyrambs with a will. Out in the woodland the gorgeous scarlet tanager announced his arrival one morning with a lively sonnet, which was heard long before the singer was seen; whereas his cousin, the summer tanager, uttered only his quaint alarm-call, "Chip-burn, chip-burn," and was excessively shy, dashing wildly away as I approached, unwilling to vouchsafe a wisp of song. Once he even pounced angrily upon his black-winged relative and drove him to the other side of the hollow, precisely as if he meant to say, "Your singing is out of place, sir, and dangerous, too! Don't you know that the man prowling about yonder will shoot little birds who betray their presence by singing?"

Northern (Baltimore) Oriole

One of our most lavish singers all summer long is the indigo bunting; yet when he first came back from the South he was very shy, and his voice seemed to be out of tune, so that, even when he tried to sing, which was seldom, his effort sounded like the creaking of a rusty door-hinge. Afterwards, however, when he got the cobwebs out of his larynx, he made up for all his previous silence. Quite different is the habit of the towhee, which announces his presence by his loud, explosive trill--all too brief--or his complaining "chewing."

Sometimes the rambler and bird gazer meets with other than avian "specimens" in his excursions. One evening I was loitering in a distant hollow, ogling with my field glass several lark sparrows that were flitting about on the ground in an adjacent patch of some kind. The birds were singing as only these beautiful sparrows can, and the quiet of the evening lent an idyllic charm to their rich and varied chansons. On the other side of a small stream stood a shanty, in the door of which sat an old negro woman. In looking at the birds, I sometimes turned the glass toward the shanty, although too intent on my studies to notice it. Presently the woman could no longer endure my apparent espionage, and so she said: "Go 'bout yer own business, mister, 'n' don' ye be spyin' inter my house!"

TROUBLE AMONG THE BIRDS*

*The larger part of this chapter was first published in "The Christian Endeavor World," Boston; the rest of it in "Our Animal Friends," New York. I reprint it here by permission of both these journals.

Even at the risk of causing a feeling of dejection on the reader's part, I am going to put one "trouble" chapter into this volume. There are trials in the birds' domain, and perhaps you and I will feel more sympathy with them, and will be led to protect them all the more carefully, if we know something about the "deep waters of affliction" through which they are sometimes compelled to pass. Our native American birds, at least some of them, suffer a good deal at the hands, so to speak, of the pestiferous English sparrows, which were introduced into this country by some egregious blunder.

There can be no doubt that the English sparrows are regular bullies. They do not fight other birds so much as they hector them, making life intolerable by their ribaldry, coarse jests, and prying manners. Some birds, especially many of our beautiful native species, are sensitively organized, and cannot endure such boorish society as the badly bred foreigners furnish. That as much as anything has driven our genteel bluebirds away from our homes into the woods and other out-of-the-way places. How would you feel, my friend, if, as you were going along the street, a lot of hoodlums should take to gibing and hooting at you?

Were there ever such pesky, ill-mannered citizens as the English sparrows? Here comes a downy woodpecker, or a cardinal, or a rose-breasted grosbeak to town, flitting about the trees of my yard, gathering goodies among the leaves and twigs, and perhaps piping a little aria at intervals, congratulating himself on having found a pleasant, quiet place, when, lo! a gang of English sparrows crowd around him, peering at him now with one eye, now with the other, canting their heads in their impertinent way, bowing and scraping and blinking, and for all the world seeming to make such derisive remarks as, "Oh, what a fine fellow! Quite stuck-up, ain't he? Isn't that a stylish topknot, though? He! he! he! Look! he wears a rose on his shirt bosom! Isn't he a dandy? Ge! ge! gah! gah!" By and by the visitor can stand the racket and the mockery no longer; and so he steals away, resolved never again to go to that place to be insulted. I have repeatedly been witness of just such occurrences.

Early in the spring a robin began to build her nest in the middle story of one of my maple trees. The whole process was narrowly watched by the noisy, hectoring sparrows. They gathered about her, prying and bobbing and jostling and chirping, staring at her like a lot of bumpkins when she leaped into the half-finished cup and molded her building material with her ruddy bosom. They seemed to be saying jeeringly: "Isn't that a funny way for a bird to build a house? Hay! hay! hay!" The robin forsook her nest; and the sparrows borrowed her timbers for their own nest, and forgot to bring them back again.

Just a moment ago a couple of young red-headed woodpeckers and their parents visited the trees of my yard, making a lively din, for the youngsters were calling for their supper. Then the sparrows crowded about them, called and jested, followed them from tree to tree, never stopping their persecutions until the red-headed family flew off in disgust.

In a Kansas town one March day, as I was returning to the house in which I was lodging, my attention was attracted to a black-capped chickadee, which was flitting about and calling in an agitated way in one of the trees. Two English sparrows, a cock and his mate, were responsible for the little bird's perturbation. What were they doing? Something rude, as usual. Perched on a couple of twigs, they were bending over, stretching out their necks and peering into a small hole in one of the larger branches. The male was especially offensive, standing there and staring into the cavity, and making insolent remarks.

A good-sized club, hurled by myself, sent the sparrows to other parts. Then I hurried into the house and sat by the curtained window to watch. With much ado, the little black-cap flew over to the limb with the cavity. He flitted about a few moments, then darted to the opening and looked in, chirping in a reassuring tone, as much as to say, "The ruffians are gone now; you can come out."

And out of the doorway flew his pretty wife, while he slipped in to see that all was safe. You see, the ill-bred sparrows had been glaring at the little madam as she sat on her nest, which was a piece of impertinence that no self-respecting bird could endure with equanimity.

The English sparrows are not the only birds that disturb the harmony of the bird realm. Offenders must needs come there as well as in the human sphere. A friend who is entirely trustworthy tells me the following story. He and his wife were driving along a country road, when their attention was directed to a kingbird in hot pursuit of a red-headed woodpecker, which had evidently been poaching on the first-named bird's preserves. Being an expert flyer, the kingbird had almost overtaken the fugitive, when suddenly the red-head wheeled to one side, flung himself somehow or other over a telegraph wire, turning at the same time and catching with his claws at the wire, where he clung, his body bent in an arc, holding his enemy at bay with his long, pointed beak and spiny tail. Of course, the martin could not attack him in that position, as he could not afford to run the risk of being impaled on the red-head's spear.

Nor was that all. The martin sailed a short distance away, and the woodpecker thought it safe to take to wing again. The kingbird again started in swift pursuit, filling the air with his loud chirping, sure of his game this time; but he was balked, as before, by the red-head's sudden dash to the telegraph wire. This little comedy was repeated several times while my friends watched with surprise and amusement.

There is tragedy as well as comedy in the world of feathers. Ernest Thompson Seton's graphic animal stories would leave a pleasanter taste in the mouth if they ended less tragically, but they would not be so true to life as it is in the faunal realm. It must be true that the lives of most birds and animals end in tragedy, so numerous, alert, and persistent are their foes. As soon as a bird begins to grow old and infirm, losing its keenness of vision and its swiftness of movement, it cannot help falling a prey to its rapacious enemies. For this reason you seldom find a feeble animal or bird in the open, or one that has lain down and died a natural death.

However, strange as it may seem, I have found the corpses of several birds in the wild outdoors. At an abandoned limestone quarry one spring I discovered the nest of a pair of phoebes. I called at the pretty domicile a number of times in my rambles. It was set on a shelf of one stratum of rock, and roofed over by another. One day I noticed the little dame sitting quietly in her cup, and decided to go near; just why, I cannot tell. She did not move as I approached; she did not even turn her head to look at me. It was strange. I went right up to the nest, and yet she did not fly. Stretching out my hand, I found that she was dead, her unhatched eggs still under her cold and pulseless bosom.

I could have wept for my little friends. There was nothing to indicate the cause of the tragedy, no disturbance of the nest, no marks of violence on her body. Possibly she had eaten or drunk poison; perhaps she had received a fatal blow from an enemy, and had just had strength enough left to come home to die. Her mate was gone. He was doubtless unable to bear the ghastly sight of his dead companion on her nest.

A little field sparrow came to a tragical end in a different way. I found his body dangling among the bushes on a bank. Two small but tough grapevine twigs growing out horizontally and close together formed a very acute angle, and this was the trap in which the innocent bird was caught. In some way one of his legs had slipped between the branches, the angle of which became more acute, of course, toward the apex. Thus the more he struggled the more tightly his tarsus became wedged in the trap, the foot preventing it from slipping through. To think of pushing his leg backward, and so releasing himself, was beyond the poor bird's cerebral power; so he fluttered until exhausted, then dangled there to die of starvation. The place being very secluded, no predatory beast or fowl had found the little corpse.

If there were only some way of protecting the nests of our beautiful and useful birds of the wildwood, what a boon it would be to men and fowls! So many nests come to grief that one wonders sometimes that any brood is ever reared. During a recent spring, with exhausting toil and patience, I found the nests of several shy woodland birds--the Kentucky, the hooded, and the creeping warblers--all of them real discoveries for me. I promised myself a rare treat in watching the development of the nurslings from babyhood to youth. Alas! all the nests were robbed, those of the Kentucky and hooded warblers of their young, and that of the creeping warbler of its eggs. I trust I am not naturally vindictive; but had I the brigands in my power who despoiled those nests, I certainly should wring their necks.

Our small birds must ever be on the qui vive. Danger is always lurking near, as a few concrete cases will show. Brush was thrown into a certain hollow well known to the writer, and one of the steep hillsides was covered with timber of a medium-sized growth. One day I was listening to a concert given by a company of towhees and cardinals, which were sitting in the trees at the lower border of the woodland. A flock of cedar waxwings were also "tseeming" in the top of a tree, darting out at intervals into the air for insects. Suddenly every song ceased, and the whole company dashed down, pellmell, hurry-skurry, into the thick brush heaps of the hollow. At the same moment, or perhaps a moment later--it all occurred so quickly I could not be exact--a covey of juncos hurled themselves with reckless swiftness into the brush pile, followed by a sparrow hawk, which uttered a queer, uncanny call that meant death to any little bird that should be overtaken.

He flung himself through a network of branches and twigs and lightly struck the ground below, his wings partly opening as he lit, to break the force of the concussion. He had dashed directly over my head. Before I could collect my wits he gathered himself together, wormed his way out through the branches in some way, and darted off up the opposite slope. He had failed to secure his prize, but it was wonderful how so large a bird could slip through the network of branches and extricate himself without striking a quill against a twig.

The extreme watchfulness of the small birds cannot fail to excite wonder in the mind of the observer. In the case just referred to not one of the birds was taken unaware, although some of them were singing gaily, and others were busy feeding. Never for a moment do the birds become so absorbed in their eating or work or play as to forget that a foe may be lurking near. One cannot help wondering how they can be happy. Suppose we were compelled to be incessantly on the lookout for danger, should we ever have a moment of peace or joy?

A red-breasted woodpecker was chiseling out a nursery in a tall sycamore at the border of a woodland. At some distance, far enough away not to alarm her, I watched the dame at her work. This was her method of procedure, hour by hour: She would plunge head first into the hole, only her barred tail being visible, give three or four vigorous dabs with her bill, then emerge and look around in every direction for danger; seeing none, into the cavity her crimson-crowned head would again disappear, only to emerge again a second later. Not for a moment did she dare to relax her vigilance. Had she done so, in that fatal moment a hawk might have swooped upon her and crushed her in his merciless talons.

Yet some birds will take not a little risk, depending on their quickness of eye and nimbleness of wing to escape their predatory foes. In a tall sycamore tree standing alone at the fringe of a piece of woodland, sparrow hawks, red-breasted woodpeckers, and nuthatches, a pair of each, had set up their household gods. The tree was still bare of foliage, for it had few branches, and the season was early spring. It was evident, too, that the hawks were watching for an opportunity to assault their neighbors, to whom they often gave chase. Yet the woodpeckers had in some way contrived to hew out their arboreal nursery, which was almost, if not quite, finished. It was a freshly chiseled cavity, as could be seen plainly from below. The mother nuthatch was feeding her young. She would fly to the tree with an insect in her bill, calling "Yank, yank," or "Ha-ha, ha-ha," as if to announce her arrival, then glide around the branch, scurry down its sloping wall, swing to the underside where the nest hole was, and jab the juicy morsel into the chirruping throat of one of the bantlings within. The bloodthirsty hawk dashed at her several times, but she deftly dodged around to the other side of the branch, and let him glide harmlessly by, flinging after him a taunting "Ha-ha, ha-ha," as much as to say, "Missed your aim again, didn't you!" However, it was a pretty picture the nuthatch made, holding in her bill a large beetle with silvery wings, sometimes holding it straight out from the bark as she glanced around to see whether the coast was clear and at the same time calling her nasal "yank," so full of woodsy suggestion.

A trying experience for many birds comes at bedtime. They grow quite nervous as night begins to settle over the land, some of them chirping loudly to express their solicitude. As the darkness deepens, their sight becomes obscured, and they seem to realize that they are exposed to dangers unseen. You have often, no doubt, noticed the to-do made by the robins as the time for retiring draws near. What foes may be lurking in the growing darkness they know not.

A favorite roosting place for the sparrows, towhees, juncos, and even the robins, was in some thickets by the roadside. As I passed along, a bird would occasionally leap from his perch to the ground and go galloping away over the rustling leaves. At one place a half dozen Harris sparrows were chirping loudly and flitting about a couple of small trees, which were partly covered with a thick network of vines. The cause of their uneasiness could not be determined, unless it was their natural fear of the darkness. I waited until night had settled. Presently the sparrows became quiet. Tramping about near the trees did not disturb them, but when I flung a lighted stick against one of the trees, they flew out of their matted bedroom with loud outcries. For a few minutes they could be seen dashing about from tree to tree; then they settled down for the night.

Northern Bobwhite Quail

In view of the many trials that naturally come into the life of the birds, we should be all the kinder to them. Why add to their sorrows? Let me give you an example of humane treatment in one case--that of the quail or bob-white. Not long ago I listened to a sensible lecturer on natural history subjects.

He did not say we should never kill the quail. They have evidently been created for man's use, or they would not have been given such juicy and nutritious flesh; just as many other fowls and animals were made to minister to the subsistence and pleasure of the human family. Besides, there can be no doubt that, if the quail were all permitted to live and multiply, they would soon become so abundant as to do much harm in our grain fields. So some of them should be killed, but not in a cruel manner.

One thing is certain, they should not be killed with shotguns! You ask at once and in some surprise, Why not? Because that is cruel. Don't you see how? Well, that is the way with most of us--we do many things without thinking. It is not cruel to kill quail with a shotgun providing they are killed outright. But have you never thought how many of the fine shot must wound some of the birds that fly away? A bird with several shots in its body may not be fatally hurt at first, but will fly off and alight somewhere in the bushes where no hunter can find it. In a few days the wounds grow sore, then gangrene sets in, and the bird slowly dies in awful torture. No one to help it, no one even to pity. Is not that cruel?

But how are these birds to be treated? They should be dealt with kindly, fed in winter, so that they will become comparatively tame, somewhat like the fowl of the barnyard. Then, in the proper season, they should be caught with a net. This can be done by placing the nets in such a way that the birds will run into them about the brush heaps, in which they are fond of taking refuge. Skill and shrewdness are needed to catch them in this way, and, perhaps, it cannot be done while they are shot at so much and are made so shy; but the time will come when the netting of quail will be regarded as rare sport in America, as hawking or fox hunting is in England.

When the birds are caught their heads should be snipped off as you do those of domestic fowls, or in some other way that is as painless as possible. According to this plan not so many birds can be secured, it is true, but it would be well to let the quail become more abundant in our country, for in certain seasons of the year they destroy certain kinds of insects that do much harm to the grain. Besides, they are such sweet and innocent birds that all of us like to see them scuttling along by the roadside, and listen to their musical calling in the clover fields--"Bob white! bob white!" Then, too, if they were allowed to become tame and plentiful, we might sometimes have the luxury of quail's eggs on our tables.

A BIRD'S EDUCATION*

*Reprinted by permission from "Forest and Stream."

So far as regards the recent discussion as to how animals learn, whether by instinct or instruction, my study of birds leads me to take a middle position; perhaps I would better say to take sides with both parties. Birds acquire knowledge partly by instinct and partly by tutelage, and the same is no doubt true of all other animals. This statement will be borne out by several concrete cases.

Some years ago I made a number of experiments in rearing young birds taken as early as possible from the nest. Among them were meadowlarks, red-winged blackbirds, brown thrashers, blue jays, wood thrushes, catbirds, flickers, red-headed woodpeckers, and several other species. Nearly all of them were secured some time before they were naturally ready to leave their natal places. Without any instruction from parents or older birds they soon left the nests I had improvised for them, hopped about on the cage floor for a while, and presently insisted on clambering upon the perches, to which they clung in the regulation way. Indeed, I noted again and again that the impulse to seek a perch was so strong that the young birds seemed to be moved to it by an imperative command. Nor were they long satisfied with a low perch, but instinctively mounted to the highest one they could find.

The same was true in regard to flight. No feathered adult was present to tutor them in the art of using their wings, yet they soon acquired that power of their own accord. It was inborn--the gift of flight. True, they were awkward at first, and gained skill only by degrees, but the original impulse was in their constitution. It is no doubt true that parent birds in the outdoors do give their young lessons in flight, but if the bantlings were left to themselves, they would acquire that art through their original endowment, although more slowly and with many more hard knocks.

As every one knows, juvenile birds at first open their mouths for their food. Proof may not be at hand for the opinion, but I am disposed to believe that they never need to be told by their parents to do that; their instincts prompt them. It must be so, I think, for to suppose that the bird baby only a day or two from the shell could understand a parental command to open its mouth would be to presume that it has the instinct to grasp the meaning of such a behest, and that is more difficult to believe than that Nature simply impels it to take its food by opening its mandibles.

Now, when the young birds are taken from the nest and reared by hand, they insist for a long time on being fed in the juvenile manner. However, by and by they begin of their own volition to pick up food after the manner of the adults. At first they are very clumsy about it, but they persevere until they acquire skill, and presently they refuse entirely to open their mandibles for food. Here again Nature is their sole guide. Without human or avian suggestion they also learn to drink in the well-known bird fashion; also to bathe, chirp, frolic, and do many other things. Who has ever seen a pet bird in drinking try to lap like a dog, or take in long draughts like a cow or a horse? No; Nature made them birds, and birds they will be. It is noticeable, too, that when birds begin to peck, or bathe, or seek a perch, they do not usually act as if they were deliberately planning to do so, nor as if they were carrying on some process of thought leading to choice, but rather as if they were impelled by Nature to do so.

The chirping of birds is mostly, if not wholly, a matter of inheritance. For instance, my little wood thrushes, as soon as they reached a sufficient age, called just like their relatives of the sylvan solitudes; my brown thrashers uttered the labial chirp of the species; my red-winged blackbird exclaimed "Chack! chack!" after the manner of his kind; my bluebirds expressed their feelings in the sad little purr of Sialia sialis; my flickers did not borrow the calls of the red-heads, but each clung to its own language; my catbirds mewed like poor pussy in trouble; and so on through the whole list. True, these pets may have heard their parents' calls before they were taken from the nest, but it is not at all likely that they would have remembered them, for at first they only "cheeped" after the manner of most bantlings, and only a good while afterward did they fall to using the adult chirp. Besides, while still in the nest, they must have heard many other bird calls; why did they not acquire them? Heredity has laid a strong hand upon birds, and has drawn sharp dividing lines among the various species.

Instinct also plays a large part in moving the bird to sing and to render the peculiar arias of its kind. For instance, a pet wood thrush of mine, secured at an early age and kept far away from all his kith of the wildwood, became a fine musician. And what do you suppose was the tune he executed? It was the sweet, dreamy, somewhat labored song of the wood thrush in his native wilds. He never sang any other tune. I think he sang it better than any wild thrush I have ever heard. It was louder, clearer, more full-toned, but the quality of voice and the technique were precisely the same. Who was his teacher? No one but Nature, heredity, instinct, whatever you choose to call it. There was no wild thrush within a half mile of his cage.

American Robin

The case of a pet thrasher was almost as striking. It is true, he may have heard several of his kin singing about the premises during the first spring of his captivity, but it is not probable that he learned their melodies so early in life. As the next spring approached, he began to sing the very medleys that the wild thrashers sing with so much earnestness and skill, and this was long before any thrashers had come back from the South.

I must now describe several cases in which inherited instinct did not prove so true a teacher. A young robin was once given me by a friend, and was kept by myself and others until the following summer. Strange as it may seem, he never acquired the well-known robin carol. Sometimes there were vague hints of it in his vocal performances, but for the most part he whistled strains in a loud, shrill tone that no wild robin ever dreamed of inflicting on the world. They were more like crude human efforts at whistling than anything else. Indeed, I think they were picked up from the whistling he heard about the house. Some of his strains were very sweet, and all of them were wonderful for a bird. A friend played "Yankee Doodle" on a cornet, and Master 'Rastus--for that was his name--gave a very fair and funny imitation of part of the air. There were many robins caroling in the trees about the premises, and 'Rastus was often left out of doors among them, but he never acquired the red-breast minstrelsy.

A similar instance was that of a pet red-winged blackbird, which, instead of whistling the labored "Grook-o-lee" of his species, learned to mimic all kinds of sounds in and out of the house, among them the crowing of the cocks of the barnyard. These two instances would indicate that some birds must at least be associated with their kin in order to learn the songs of their species.

My comical pet blue jay gave proof of the need of parental training. While he intuitively called like a jay, he never was able to sing the sweet, gurgling roulade of the wild jays. On the contrary, he treated us to all kinds of odd, imitative, mirth-provoking performances that no self-respecting jay in the open would think of enacting. After several months of cage life he was given his liberty. Now, indeed, he showed his lack of jay bringing up, and how little, in some respects, mere instinct can be relied on. When evening came he perched on a limb of the maple tree before the house, in a place as exposed as he could well find, not knowing that there was more danger in an outdoor roost than in his shielding cage. I could not induce him to come down, nor could I climb out to the branch on which he sat, and so I was compelled to leave him out of doors.

The next morning he was safe, the screech owls of the neighborhood having overlooked him in some way. The next evening he went to roost in the same exposed place, and that was the last I ever saw of my beloved pet. He was undoubtedly killed and devoured by the owls. Had he been reared out of doors in the usual way, his parents would have taught him to find a roosting place that was secure from predatory foes. No one has ever seen a wild jay sleeping in an exposed place.

In her charming little book, "True Bird Stories," Mrs. Olive Thorne Miller says that she "once watched the doings in a crow nursery." I quote:
"The most important thing the elders had to do was to teach the youngsters how to fly, and every little while one or both of the parents would fly around the pasture, giving a peculiar call as they went. This call appeared to be an order to the little folks to follow, for all would start up and circle round for a minute or two, and then drop back to the fence or the ground to rest.

"Once, while I was watching them, this cry was given, and all flew as usual except one bob-tailed baby, who stood on a big stone in the middle of the field. He was perhaps so comfortable that he did not want to go, or it may be he was afraid, and thought mamma would not notice him. But mothers' eyes are sharp, and she did see him. She knew, too, that baby crows must learn to fly; so when all came down again she flew right at the naughty bird, and knocked him off his perch. He squawked, and fluttered his wings to keep from falling, but the blow came so suddenly that he had not time to save himself, and he fell flat on the ground. In a minute he clambered back upon his stone, and I watched him closely. The next time the call came to fly he did not linger, but went with the rest, and so long as I could watch him he never disobeyed again."

This is evidence not only of parental teaching, but also of parental discipline. Here is another bit from the same volume, bearing its lesson on its face. "A lady told me a funny story about a robin. He was brought up in the house from the nest, and never learned to sing the robin song, for he had not heard it. He plainly tried to make some sort of music, and one of the family taught him to whistle 'Yankee Doodle'. He whistled it perfectly, and never tried to sing anything else. Once this Yankee Doodle robin got out of the house and flew up into a tree. When the wild birds came about him he entertained them by whistling his favorite air, which sent the birds off in a panic."

Do not the facts recited in this sketch prove that birds know and acquire some things through the promptings of instinct, while other things they can learn only by avian teaching?

My notes on instinct and education in bird song correspond with the conviction expressed by Dr. W. H. Hudson on page 257 of his interesting book entitled "The Naturalist in La Plata," fourth edition, 1903: "It is true that Daines Barrington's notion that young song birds learn to sing only by imitating the adults, still holds its ground; and Darwin gives it his approval in his 'Descent of Man'. It is perhaps one of those doctrines which are partly true, or which do not contain the whole truth; and it is possible to believe that, while many singing birds do so learn their songs, or acquire a greater proficiency in them from hearing the adults, in other species the song comes instinctively, and is, like other instincts and habits, purely an 'inherited memory'." What Dr. Hudson surmises may be the case, I believe my experiments have proved to be true.

ARE BIRDS SINGERS OR WHISTLERS?*

*Reprinted by permission from "Our Animal Friends."

Not a little discussion has arisen among the dissectors as to the anatomy of bird song. Into this controversy I shall not enter--at least, not in a controversial spirit--but shall recount only what may be regarded as the best and latest results of scientific research. How does a bird produce the melodious notes that emanate from his throat? Are they manufactured far down in the trachea, or only at its anterior opening? Are they voice tones or flute tones? These questions will be answered as we proceed to examine the bird's lyrical apparatus without going into wearisome detail, or making use of many difficult scientific terms, which are the bane of the general reader.

Let me begin at the upper end of the avian singing machine--that is, with the mouth, including the bill, the lips of which are called mandibles. Just as the movements of the human lips have much to do with the modifications of the human voice, so the opening and closing of the bird's mandibles exercise a modifying influence upon avicular tones. If it were not so, the feathered minstrel would not keep his mandibles in such constant motion during his lyrical recitals. You will notice that whenever he desires to strike a very high and loud note he opens his mandibles quite widely, sometimes almost to the fullest possible extent.

However, the expansion and contraction of the throat orifice, no doubt, produce still more marked variations in the tones of the vocalist; yet it must be borne in mind that closed or partly closed mandibles will obstruct the passage of the air from the throat, while open mandibles will permit of a full passage of the air current, and the tones will vary accordingly. Besides, the roof of the bird's mouth is grooved or convex, and therefore the character of the sounds will be somewhat dependent upon the position and movement of the upper mandible.

And then there is the bird's tongue, which is constantly in motion while the musical rehearsal is going on. Throughout its entire length it can be raised and lowered at the bird's will, or be made to quiver and roll, and by this means the air column forced up from the lungs is manipulated in a wonderful way, producing in some cases an almost unlimited variety of modulation.

Within the bird's neck two elastic tubes run down from the mouth into the chest. One of them is the gullet or aesophagus, which is the channel through which the bird's food descends into the crop and gizzard. The other little cylinder lies in front of the gullet, and is called the windpipe or trachea, and reaches down to the lungs, which are the bellows furnishing the wind for the avian pipe organ. As Dr. Coues says, the trachea is "composed of a series of very numerous gristly or bony rings connected together by an elastic membrane," and is supplied with an intricate set of muscles by which it can be shortened or elongated at the will of the songster himself.

Now let us look at the upper end of this wonderful pneumatic pipe, which so often throws Pan and all his coterie into a transport when the thrasher and the wood thrush flute their dithyrambs. Here we find the larynx. It is simply the anterior specialized portion of the trachea, located at the base of the tongue, and in mammals is honored as the voice organ, whereas in birds it is distinguished as the fluting apparatus, the instrument that really produces the varied vocalization of the bird realm. But the music is not the product of vocal cords, as is the case in the human larynx, for at the upper end of the avian larynx there is a slit or fissure, somewhat elliptical in form, and set in the fork of the hyoid bone, which constitutes the bifurcated root of the tongue. This fissure is called the glottis. At the bird's fiat, it can be opened and closed and made to assume a great variety of forms. Moreover, just in front of it there is a fold of mucous membrane called the epiglottis, which is in reality a tiny trapdoor closing over the opening when necessity requires. When the bird swallows food or drink, this little flap shuts down, and prevents the entrance of any clogging substance into the windpipe to choke the feathered diner.

We have now come to the most strategic point in our investigation of the anatomy of bird song, for in the avian world a special distinction has been conferred upon that little orifice in the bird's throat called the glottis. It is here that all the music, as well as all other so-called vocal sounds, are generated--they are simply piped or fluted through a slit, so that birds are whistlers, not singers or vocalists. I repeat, so that my meaning may be perfectly clear--bird music is not produced by means of vocal cords, as is the music of the human throat, but by means of a whistling aperture in the larynx. And that wonderful cleft has been placed there for that specific purpose. Properly speaking, therefore, the feathered choralist does not have a voice, but only a wind instrument; albeit a marvelous contrivance it is.

It will be easy now to see how the bird's tones are capable of a large variety of modulations. The glottis is controlled by a system of muscles that are perfectly obedient, within their limits, to the bird's volitions, and thus it may be made to assume a great number of different forms, each giving expression to a different vocal effect. The shape of the glottis is also modified in numerous ways by the movement of the tongue and mandibles. Nor is that all, for the air column pumped up from the lungs may be increased or diminished at will, a very strong current producing a loud tone, and a feeble current a low one. The elongation or contraction of the whole throat will also modify the pneumatic column, and thereby alter the quality of the tones.

We may go still further in our analysis. Suppose a bird should open his mouth and throat as widely as possible, hold all his lyrical organs steady, and blow his windpipe with all the strength his lungs could command, it is obvious that the effect would be a clear, loud, uniform whistle, such as the meadowlark sends across the green fields. But suppose he desires to "blow a dreamy hautbois note, slender and refined as ever stirred the air of Arcady or trembled in the vineyards of old Provence," then all the musician in plumes needs to do is to contract the slit in his throat, depress his tongue, almost close his mandibles, and simply allow a slender air current to sift from the lungs through the syrinx and out of the glottis. What if the whim should seize him to pipe a trill or a quaver to the water witches of the meadow, as Master Song Sparrow so often chooses to do? Then he simply needs to set his tongue and throat to quivering, and you have his enrapturing tremolo. Beautiful, is it not?

There are birds that send a kind of guttural sound from their throats, such as the cuckoos and occasionally the blue jays. Notice the cuckoo as he utters his call, which every swain interprets as the harbinger of a coming shower, and you will observe that his throat bulges out like that of a croaking frog, and quivers at the same time in a convulsed way. It is plain that the air about to be forced from the glottis is flung back by some muscular action and set to vibrating in the laryngean cavity, thus giving the sound its croaking quality when the elastic current is finally released.

Now, if the reader will pucker up his lips and whistle a tune, he will notice that the sound is actually produced at the small labial orifice and nowhere else; however, the tones are modified and modulated at will in a variety of ways--by a deft, though almost imperceptible, manipulation of the tongue, by a slight enlargement or contraction of the aperture, and especially by a dexterous control of the air column blown from the lungs. Just so the lyrists of fields and woods pipe their roundels and chansons through the chink in their throats, save that in the bird's case the mouth and tongue are anterior to the whistling aperture. I know a young man who has trained himself so as to be able to mimic to perfection the complex songs of the western meadowlark and the cardinal grosbeak. He does it by whistling.

Near the lower end of the trachea, just above the lungs, there is a specialized organ of the bird's throat called the syrinx. It is a cylinder formed of bony rings, provided with a mesh of muscles, and having membranous folds which act as valves upon the two orifices of the bronchi leading to the lungs. Many scientific gentlemen have declared that the syrinx is the voice organ of the birds, the elastic margins of the folds or valves being set to vibrating by the projection of the air from the lungs, and thus producing the varied lays we hear in the outdoor concert. However, Mr. Maurice Thompson--who, by the way, found time to do something else besides writing "Alice of Old Vincennes," and something just as creditable to his talent, too--dissected many birds with special reference to this subject, and gave close attention to birds in the act of singing, both out of doors and in captivity, and I am convinced that he proved the theory of the syringeal origin of bird song to be an erroneous one.

Only two reasons need be adduced for this conclusion. First, it is unreasonable to suppose that the rich, loud, clear notes of the thrasher, the cardinal, and the mockingbird, lilting across the fields and capable of being heard a long distance, are generated far down in the lyrist's chest by the vibrating of the margin of a tiny mucous membrane. If it had its genesis there, it surely would display a muffled or guttural or sepulchral quality. In the second place, it has been proved by actual dissection that the shrike, which possesses no song gift worthy of the name, has a well-developed syrinx, while the mockingbird, our feathered minstrel par excellence, has a syrinx that is absolutely insignificant. On the other hand, the shrike's larynx, including the glottis, is a clumsy affair, whereas the mocker's larynx is indeed wonderfully made.

Western Meadowlark

It must not be supposed, however, that the syrinx does not perform an important function in the production of avian melody. It acts as a regulator or meter of the air impelled from the lungs. By means of the folds or membranous valves the mouths of the bronchial tubes may be opened widely or almost closed, and in this way, to quote from Mr. Thompson, "the bird is enabled to measure in the nicest manner the amount of air thrown from the lungs into the trachea." In producing a staccato, for example, the valves flop up and down, doling out the air at the proper intervals and in precisely the right quantities.

Indeed, nothing in the world of Nature is more wonderful than the gift of bird song, and nothing proves more clearly the doctrine of design, or, at least, of adaptation to a specialized purpose.

BIRD FLIGHT*

*Reprinted by permission from "The Evening Post," New York.

The question why man cannot fly may be answered in a very simple and yet satisfactory manner: He has not been organically constructed for that purpose. That may seem like cutting the Gordian knot, but, after all, it is the only explanation that can be given. You might as well ask why man cannot clutch a perch with his foot after the manner of a bird or a monkey, for the response would be the same--his foot was made for walking, and not for prehensile purposes. On the other hand, the bird cannot grasp an object with its wings, while a man's hand is well adapted for the performance of such a function. Nature's motto in her whole realm seems to be: "Every creature after its kind."

When we look at the structure of the flying birds, we see at once that they were formed for swift locomotion through the air, just as plainly as the lithe skiff was made to glide over the water or the carriage to spin over the land. In the first place, the body of the bird is comparatively light--that is, in proportion to the width, strength, and extent of its wings. By its thick, light, airy covering of feathers its body is made still more buoyant, besides presenting a larger surface to the supporting air with very little additional weight. The tail, too, with its long, closely woven quills spread out like a fan, not only serves the purpose of a rudder for guiding the aerial craft, but is still more useful in helping to sustain the bird's weight in the up-buoying element.

It is interesting to note that the feathers on the bodies of the flying birds are arranged in tracts, with intervals here and there of quite, or almost, bare skin, called "apteria." Now, when a bird is carefully skinned, it will be seen that the feathered spaces have their own special slips of muscles inserted into the roots of the feathers, and when these muscles are contracted, they serve to raise the feathers, and must, therefore, be of some subsidiary value in flying, by making the bird's body more buoyant. Suggestive, indeed, is the fact that the plumes of the non-flyers are not arranged in tracts, but are evenly distributed over the body.

Nor is that all that Nature has done to carry out her evident purpose of making the bird a natural "flying machine." The body of the bird contains numerous air sacs, all connected with the lungs, and these, when inflated, are a great help in flying by making the bird light. More than that, many of the bones, though strong, have thin walls and are hollow, the cavities being connected with the lungs and air sacs, from which they are also filled with air, contributing another element of lightness to the aerial navigator. That the bird's bones are capable of being permeated with air can be demonstrated by actual experiment, and is, therefore, a scientifically established fact. It is easy enough to prove it in this way: Take a dead bird that has been beheaded, pass a syringe into its windpipe, tie it carefully so that the air cannot escape at the sides, then blow the air down through the tube, and you will be able to follow the passage of the air into the skin and other parts of the body. Now, if you will cut off one of the bones, you can detect the air passing from the cut surface; and, more than that, as a scientific English writer says, "if the experiment be made by using colored fluid instead of air--which is pumped in by a syringe--the fluid can be seen to ooze from the ends of any bone or muscle that has been cut across." Thus it is seen that the whole body of the fowl is so constructed that it can be pervaded with air.

However, while all parts of the bird's organism combine to produce the end in view, the special instruments of flight are the wings. They are really the fore limbs of the fowl, but differ in many respects from the fore limbs of the mammals. They are under the control of muscles of great comparative strength, as every one knows who has ever been beaten by the wings of even an ordinary barnyard fowl, which has meagre powers of flight. What a powerful stroke a large hawk or an eagle must be able to deliver! If man's arm muscles were as strong in proportion, he might have some hope of one day navigating the air on artificial wings, but it is due principally to this muscular weakness that Darius Green has never been able to make a success of his flying machine, and perhaps never will. He would not have the strength to wield wings large enough to sustain so much avoirdupois on the yielding air.

The wings are highly specialized members of the avicular organism, and hence differ in many important respects from the fore or pectoral limbs of the mammals. Beginning at the point nearest the body, let us examine one of these wonderful instruments. The wing proper begins at the shoulder joint, which hinges freely upon the shoulder in a shallow socket, into which the globular head of the first bone fits closely, and in which it is firmly held by the powerful muscles that control the organs of flight. The first bone is called the humerus, and is the largest and strongest bone of the wing, extending from the shoulder to the elbow. At the elbow, which is the first angle of the wing, reaching backward when the wing is folded, the humerus articulates in a wisely designed way with two other bones, called the ulna and radius, which together constitute the forearm and extend to the wrist joint. It must be remembered that, when the wing is closed, the forearm is the segment that reaches obliquely forward. The wrist joint is the second angle of the wing. In the wrist there are two small bones (the radiale and ulnare) which serve an important purpose in joining the forearm with what is known as the hand, and make possible the specialized movement of the two parts upon each other. The hand is the terminal segment of the wing, composed of the metacarpal bones and the digits or fingers. Of the last-named organs there are ordinarily three, forming a graceful tapering point to the wing, and giving to it the symmetry and proportion that are required for effective use. When the wing is folded, the hand extends obliquely downward and backward.

Now, these bones and their attendant ligatures are wonderfully and wisely contrived. The humerus moves freely in its socket in the shoulder, so that it can be swung in every required direction, and yet, as should be the case, its principal movement is up and down in a vertical line--the precise movement required for the effective wingstrokes in flight. But note further. The elbow joint, unlike that of the shoulder, is a rigid hinge, permitting motion in only one plane, that of the wing itself, or nearly so. The same is true of the wrist joint, which holds the hand firmly, allowing no motion save that which opens and closes the wing. The wisdom of this arrangement will be seen at a glance.

In the human arm the hand can be moved in every direction with the greatest freedom, and, moreover, the wrist may be turned and the hand laid on its back, its palm, its edge, or at almost any conceivable angle. This is a very convenient contrivance for man, but it would be a great misfortune for our avian friends if their wings would rotate so readily; for in that case they would not have sufficient rigidity to answer the purposes of flight, but would be twisted into every position by the assaults of the air currents. Besides, even in ordinary flight it would require a constant muscular effort to keep the wings in the proper position. How wisely Nature has devised the bird's flying apparatus! When outstretched, it is held firmly by the power of its own mechanism, with its broad under surface lying horizontally, and no breezy current can bend or twist it from its normal position.

The set of muscles that open the wing are called the extensors, and those that close it, the flexors. The former lie upon the back of the upper arm and the front of the forearm and the hand, their tendons passing over the convexities of the elbow and wrist, while the flexors occupy the opposite sides, and their tendons run up into the concavities of the joints. There are several powerful pectoral muscles which run out from the shoulder and breast, and operate upon the upper end of the humerus, and with these the wing is lifted and the strokes are made during flight.

Another mechanical contrivance deserves attention. An extremely elastic cord reaches over from the shoulder to the wrist joint, supporting a fold of skin that occupies the deep angle of the elbow, and that is covered with short, fluffy feathers. When the bird is flying, this cord is stretched and forms the front edge of that section of the wing. But, now, suppose the wing is closed, will not this cord make a cumbersome fold, flapping loosely in the angle of the elbow? Such would, indeed, be the case, did not its extreme elasticity enable it to contract to the proper length, so as to keep the wing's border straight and smooth.

Without the feathers the wing would be useless as an instrument of flight. The shorter plumes that shield the bases of the long quill feathers are called the coverts, which are found on both the upper and under surfaces of the wing. They are divided into several sets, according to the position they occupy, and are called the "primary coverts" (because they overlie the bases of the primaries), the "greater coverts," the "middle coverts," and the "lesser coverts." Forming a vast expansion of the bony and fleshy framework are the quills, or flight-feathers, called collectively the "remiges." These plumes mainly determine the contour of the wing, and constitute a thin, elastic surface for striking the air--one that is sufficiently resilient to give the proper rebound and yet firm enough to support the bird's weight. The longest quills are those that grow on the hand or outer extremity of the wing and are known as the primaries. What are called the secondaries are attached to the ulna of the forearm, while the tertiaries occupy the humerus and are next to the body. All these feathers are so placed relatively that the stiff outer vane of each quill overlaps the more flexible inner vane of its successor, like the leaves of certain kinds of fans, thus presenting an unbroken surface to the air. As to the structure of these plumes, they combine firmness, lightness, and mobility, the barbs and barbules knitting the more flexible parts together, so that they do not separate, but only expand, when the wing is unfolded.

Barn Swallow

While the primary purpose of wings is flight, there is quite a number of notable exceptions. A concrete example is the ostrich, whose wings are too feeble to lift it from the ground, but evidently aid the great fowl in running, as it holds them outspread while it skims over the plain, perhaps using them mainly as outriggers or balancing poles in its swift passage on its stilt-like legs. The penguins convert their wings into fins while swimming through the water, the feathers closely resembling scales.

There are birds of many kinds, and therefore a great variety of wings and modes of flight. Birds with short, broad, rounded wings, with the under surface slightly concave and the upper surface correspondingly convex, usually have comparatively heavy bodies, and race through the air with rapid wing-beats and rather labored flight, and compass only short distances. Among the birds of this kind of aerial movement may be mentioned the American meadowlark, the bob-white, and the pheasant. Other species propel themselves in rapid, gliding, and continued flight by means of long, narrow, and pointed wings, like the swifts, swallows, and goatsuckers, while many others, notably herons, hawks, vultures, and eagles, are distinguished by a vast alar expansion in proportion to their weight, and hence are able to sustain themselves in the air by sailing, with only a slight stroke at rare intervals. Such birds as the stormy petrel and the frigate-bird have wings that are broad, convex, and of great length in contrast with the lightness and small bulk of their bodies, for which reason they are able to sustain themselves in the air for days without rest. It is even thought that some of these wonderful birds of the limitless ocean sleep on the wing, though how such an hypothesis could be proved it would be difficult to say.

Even in this day of scientific research and astuteness, it must not be supposed that everything about the mechanics of avicular flight is understood. We may readily comprehend how a bird, without fluttering its wings, can poise in the air; but how can it move forward or in a circle, and even mount upward, without a visible movement of a pinion? And this some birds are able to do without reference to the direction of the ethereal currents. That, I venture to say, is still a mystery. It almost seems as if some of the masters of aerial navigation in the bird world were gifted with the ability to propel themselves forward by a mere act of volition.

An interesting article on the subject of bird flight appeared not long ago in one of the foremost periodicals of the country, a part of which is here quoted to show what a puzzling problem we have before us:

Recent developments in aerial navigation have renewed interest in the comparative study of the mechanical principles involved in the flying of birds. There is one exceedingly puzzling law in regard to birds and all flying creatures, the solution of which may work far-reaching influences in the construction of flying craft.

"This law, which has thus far perplexed scientists, is that the heavier and bigger the bird or insect, the less relative wing area is required for its support. Thus the area of wing surface of a gnat is forty-nine units of area to every one of weight. In graphic contrast to that, a condor (Sarcorhamphus gryphus) which weighed 16.52 pounds had a wing surface of 9.80 square feet. In other words, though the gnat needs wing surface in a ratio of forty-nine square feet per pound of weight, a great condor manages to sail along majestically with .59 of a square foot to at least a pound of weight. The unexplained phenomenon persists consistently throughout the whole domain of entomology and ornithology. Going up the scale from the gnat, it is found that with the dragon fly this ratio is 30 to 1, with the tipula, or daddy-longlegs, 14.5 to 1, the cockchafer only 5.15 to 1, the rhinoceros beetle 3.14 to 1.

"Among birds the paradoxical law that the smaller the creature the bigger the relative supporting wings holds good. A screech owl (Scops zorca) weighing one-third of a pound had 2.35 square feet of wing surface per pound of weight. A fish hawk (Pandion haliaetus) weighing nearly three pounds had a wing area of 1.08 square feet to each pound. A turkey buzzard weighing 5.6 pounds had a little less than one square foot of wing surface to each pound. A griffon vulture (Gyps fulvus) weighing 16.52 pounds had a wing surface of only .68 square feet to the pound.

"Students of aerial navigation who are devoting much attention to observations of birds say that if the peculiar law governing extant flying creatures could be fathomed the problem of human flight might be solved."

A BIRD'S FOOT

You will agree with me, after you have studied a bird's foot, that it is one of Nature's most wonderful contrivances, so admirably adapted for the purposes to which it is devoted that one cannot help feeling that a Divine Mind must have planned it, just as a man would make a watch for the express purpose of keeping time.

But what is properly included in a bird's foot? Here we shall have to correct a popular mistake, if we wish to be accurate, in the scientific sense of the term. Most people think that the avian foot consists only of the toes and claws, or the part that comes in direct contact with the ground or the perch. That, however, is an error, for the foot really comprises, in addition to the toes and claws, the first long bone of the limb, reaching from the base of the digits to the first joint. You will see, therefore, that the bird walks on its toes, not on its foot as a whole.

The long bone referred to--called the tarsus--corresponds to the instep of the human foot, that is, the foot proper, while the joint which extends backward, forming an angle with the next large bone, is really the bird's heel. Thus you perceive that most birds walk with their heels high in the air. What most people call the bird's "leg" is in reality the bird's foot, and what they call its "foot" comprises only its toes and claws.

To obtain a correct idea of the bird's entire walking apparatus, we begin with the uppermost part of the leg. As we proceed, it would be well to keep in mind the different parts of the human leg and foot. The highest bone is called the thigh bone or femur, which is, for the most part, enclosed in the general integument of the body, and is not entirely separate from it as is the thigh bone of the human leg. Among carvers it is known as the "second joint." It reaches forward and slightly downward, and is hidden under the feathers of the body. The upper end of the femur enlarges into a globular head, which fits into the socket of the hip in the pelvis, while the lower end meets another long bone, which extends obliquely backward and downward and with which it forms the knee joint.

The knee of the bird extends forward, as the human knee does when it is bent. By means of various nodules and tendons the femur is articulated with and fastened to the next large bone at the knee joint. This second bone is the leg proper, called in scientific language the crus. When, with its thick, palatable flesh, it is cooked and placed on the table, it is known as the "drumstick"--a favorite part of the fowl with hungry boys, vying, in their minds, with the "white meat" of the breast.

This important segment of the limb is composed of two bones, the larger of which is called the tibia, the smaller the fibula. At its lower end the tibia forms what is known as the ankle joint by articulating with the next long bone, which is commonly called the tarsus, although the proper name would be really metatarsus. It is not often that this bone is covered with flesh, and therefore it seldom finds its way to the table. Properly speaking, it is the larger part of the bird's foot, reaching obliquely upward and backward from the roots of the toes to the heel. If you will lift yourself upon your toes, holding your heels in the air, you will be able to form a correct idea of what the bird is doing whenever it stands or walks or perches.

The toes are fastened by means of well adapted joints to the lower end of the tarsus, and form what is popularly regarded as the bird's foot. When spoken of separately, these toes are called digits, and when spoken of collectively, they are called the podium. They are composed of small bones called phalanges or internodes, which are jointed upon one another like the several parts of the human fingers. The digits can be spread out for walking purposes, or bent around so as to clasp an object. The outer bone of each digit almost always bears a nail or claw, which is sometimes very strong and hooked, as is the case with the birds of prey, while in other species it is only slightly curved and is not meant as a weapon of offense or defense, but chiefly to enable the bird to "scratch for a living."

How do the birds, in perching and roosting, retain their hold so long on a limb without becoming weary? They do not need to make a conscious effort to do this, but are held by the mechanical action of certain muscles and tendons in the leg and foot. Of course, the bird can also control these muscles by an act of its will, but a large part of their action is automatic. In some species there is a muscle called the ambiens, which has its rise in the pelvis, passes along the inner side of the thigh, whence its tendon runs over the apex of the angle of the knee joint, and down the leg till it joins the muscles that flex the toes. Now when the bird's leg is bent at the joints, as is the case in perching, the tendons of this muscle are stretched over the knee and ankle joints, thus pulling the digits together, and causing them of their own accord to grasp the perch more or less tightly. When a bird wishes to unloose its hold, it simply rises on its feet and relaxes the tendons.

All birds by no means possess this particular muscle, but all the perchers have some muscular arrangement in the legs and toes that practically answers the same purpose. If you will bend your wrist backward as far as you can, you will observe that your fingers will have a tendency to curve slightly forward. This is caused by the stretching of the tendons over the convex part of your bent wrist joints.

The typical bird has four digits, three in front and one reaching backward. The hind toe is called the hallux, and corresponds to the thumb of the human hand, so that in grasping an object it can be made to meet any of the other toes. But many birds are not provided with a quartet of digits. The ostrich has only two, the inner and hinder toes being wanting. However, this great fowl does not experience any lack, for its feet are almost solid like hoofs, and quite flat, and hence are especially adapted for traveling across the sandy desert.

No bird has ever been found with more than four toes; and four seem to be ample for all purposes. A fifth toe for a bird would be as useless as a fifth wheel on a wagon. Quite a number of species have only three toes, most of them among the walkers and waders, and none, I believe, among the true perchers. Take the plovers and sanderlings, for example, which spend most of their time, when not on the wing, in running about on the ground, especially along the seashore or the banks of streams and lakes, and seldom, if ever, sit on a perch--in their case a fourth toe would be worse than a superfluous appendage; it would be an encumbrance, dragging along in the mud and mire. In these species it is the hind toe that is lacking, their three digits all being in front, where they are of the greatest service. There is another class of birds that have hind toes, though very much reduced because their owners do not perch, but scuttle about on the beach. This class includes the little spotted sandpipers which you often see running or flying along the shores of a river or lake.

Curious to tell, several species of woodpeckers are tridactyl--that is, three-toed--and still more curious is the fact that in their case the true hind toe is lacking, while the outer front toe is bent backward, or "reversed," as it is called, and is thus made to do service for a hind toe. The other species of woodpeckers have four toes, two in front and two behind, the outer one of the latter pair being a reversed digit. Why some of the woodpeckers should have four toes and others only three is an unsolved enigma, and is especially puzzling in view of the fact that the four-toed kinds do not seem to possess any advantage over their cousins. The tridactyl species are as expert climbers as any members of the family, and are extremely hardy birds, too, some of them dwelling the year round in cold northern climates, where the food question must often be a serious one.

Spotted Sandpiper

Here is still another conundrum for the bird student: Why do the four-toed woodpeckers have two hind digits, despite the fact that they always clamber upward when they take their promenades on the boles and branches of the trees, whereas the agile little nuthatch, which glides upward or downward, as the impulse moves him, has only one rear toe and three in front, like the true perchers? Nor is it less puzzling that the cuckoos, which are perching birds, should have two toes in front and two behind. Then, there is the little brown creeper which never perches and is forever creeping, creeping, upward, upward--save, of course, when it takes to wing--and yet its toes are arranged in the normal percher style, the hind digit having an especially long, curved claw. It is a mistake to suppose that all the problems of the bird world have been solved.

Look at the different kinds of birds' feet and see how wisely they have been planned for the various purposes to which they have been applied. In order that a bird may use his feet with the greatest dexterity in perching and flitting, his digits should be as free and movable as possible; and so we find that the toes of the perchers are usually cleft to the base, are long and slender, easily opened and closed, and possess the power to grasp an object firmly. The same is true of the raptorial birds, or birds of prey, which are strong perchers and depend largely for their food supply on clutching their victims while on the wing. In all these birds the hind toe is also well developed, and is on the same plane as the anterior digits--a wise adaptation of means to ends.

But there are other birds whose feet, as some one has said, are good feet, but poor hands--that is, they are not intended for prehensile purposes, only for walking and wading. Therefore, in these birds the hind toe is small, and more or less elevated above the plane of the other digits, or, as has already been said, is wholly wanting. The feet of some of these birds are partly webbed, so that, if necessary, they can change their mode of locomotion from running and wading to swimming. Birds whose feet are partly webbed are said to be semipalmated.

This introduces us to that interesting group of birds whose toes are connected throughout their entire length by a thin, membranous web. Their feet are said to be palmated. We can readily understand why they are thus formed, for their webbed feet answer the purpose of oars to propel them over the water. Most of the swimmers have feet of this kind. Watch them glide like feathered craft over the smooth surface of the stream or lake.

When a swimmer thrusts his foot forward, the toes naturally drop together and partly close, presenting only a narrow front--almost an edge--of resistance to the water; then, when he makes a backward stroke, the toes spread far apart and, with the connecting membranes, are converted into a broad, propelling oar. Is it not a wonderfully wise contrivance?

Most swimming birds have only the front toes webbed, but in a few species, like the pelicans, even the hind toe is connected with its fellows by means of such a membrane. Nor must we forget those water fowls which, instead of palmated feet, have what is called the lobate foot, which means that the digits have broad lobes or flaps on their sides. While in such cases the toes are all distinct, the expanded lobes serve almost, if not quite, as good a purpose for propulsion in the water as do the webs. The coot swims almost as well as the duck or the goose, and at the same time his feet, with their disconnected toes, are better adapted for paddling about amid the watergrass and dense weeds than if they were webbed.

The birds of prey, such as hawks, owls, and eagles, have large, strong, and sharply curved talons and powerful digits, and a sad use they make of them in clutching small birds and animals. The claws of the woodpeckers and other climbing birds are stout and extremely acute, just as they should be for clinging to the bark of trees. In short, the structure of a bird's foot, whatever may be the species of fowl, furnishes most conclusive evidence of adaptation in the world of Nature.

THE END

www.ingramcontent.com/pod-product-compliance
Lightning Source LLC
Chambersburg PA
CBHW070434290526
45791CB00005B/1967